CW00923260

"In the Name of Allāh, the Most Beneficent,
the Most Merciful"

Contents

Contents

Introduction

All praises are due to Allāh ﷻ. May peace, salutations and blessings be upon our guide and mentor, the final and beloved Prophet
Muhammad ﷺ, upon his noble Sahābahs ﵃, Tābi'een and those
who follow their noble lifestyles until the Day of Judgement.
Āmeen!

The life of this world is only for a short period of time and a test
for humanity. Unfortunately, many individuals, males and fe-
males forget this and they focus all their energy and resources in
attaining the 'pleasures' of this world. It soon becomes a contest
between some individuals to see who has more and the best
worldly assets.

In the Holy Qur'ān, Allāh ﷻ compares the life of this world to a
flower. A flower starts its life as an insignificant tiny
seed. Through the necessary minerals and nutrients, the seed
slowly starts growing until it blosoms into a beautiful flower. After some time, the once beautiful, sweet smelling flower begins to
slowly wilt and crumble away. This can be compared to a man
who starts his life in a helpless state (child), and through the Grace
of Allah ﷻ, he begins to mature and gain strength and intelligence
in the process of his/her life and experiences. Thereafter, he begins to deteriorate through old age and illnesses, hence, slowly
losing the strength and intelligence he once had and his physical
features starts diminishing too. That is why, as Muslims we must

do things that will be of benefit to us in the Hereafter as everyone, Muslim or non-Muslim, shall face death.

In this book, 'The End of Time,' my beloved Shaykh and teacher, Mufti Saiful Islām Sāhib explains the different processes in preparing for the Final Day, the Judgement Day and the conditions of those who are in Jannah and Jahannam through the comprehensive commentary of Sūrah Takweer, Sūrah Infitār and Sūrah Mutaffifeen. These three beautiful Sūrahs are connected as they have a common theme, the end of time, the Hereafter, the Judgement Day. The three Sūrahs also explain when and how the end of time will occur and that every person, male or female will see on that Day whatever he/she has done in the world.

May Allāh ﷻ protect us from the hardships and torments of that Final Day! May Allāh ﷻ accept the efforts of all those who have participated in the writing and compilation of this book, especially my beloved teacher and Shaykh, Mufti Saiful Islām Sāhib and reward them in the life of this world and the Hereafter. Āmeen!

Maulāna Ismāeel Aziz
Graduate of JKN
November 2016 / Safar 1438

Sūrah Takweer

The Folding
Revealed in Makkah

بِسْمِ اللهِ الرَّحْمٰنِ الرَّحِيمِ

In the Name of Allāh, the Most Compassionate, the Most Merciful

إِذَا الشَّمْسُ كُوِّرَتْ . وَإِذَا النُّجُومُ انْكَدَرَتْ . وَإِذَا الْجِبَالُ سُيِّرَتْ . وَإِذَا الْعِشَارُ عُطِّلَتْ . وَإِذَا الْوُحُوشُ حُشِرَتْ . وَإِذَا الْبِحَارُ سُجِّرَتْ . وَإِذَا النُّفُوسُ زُوِّجَتْ . وَإِذَا الْمَوْءُودَةُ سُئِلَتْ . بِأَيِّ ذَنْبٍ قُتِلَتْ . وَإِذَا الصُّحُفُ نُشِرَتْ . وَإِذَا السَّمَاءُ كُشِطَتْ . وَإِذَا الْجَحِيمُ سُعِّرَتْ . وَإِذَا الْجَنَّةُ أُزْلِفَتْ . عَلِمَتْ نَفْسٌ مَّا أَحْضَرَتْ

1. When the sun loses its light.
2. When the stars fall down.
3. When the mountains are made to fly about.
4. When pregnant camels are forsaken.
5. When wild animals are gathered.
6. When the oceans are set alight.
7. When the souls are joined.
8. When the girl buried alive will be asked.
9. For what sin she was killed?
10. When the records of deeds will be opened.
11. When the sky will be opened.
12. When Jahannam will be fuelled.
13. When Jannah will be brought close.

14. On that Day, every soul will know what deeds it had presented.

Imām Ahmad ﷺ recorded from Sayyidunā Abdullāh Ibn Umar ﷺ that the Holy Prophet ﷺ said,

مَنْ سَرَّهُ أَنْ يَّنْظُرَ إِلَى الْقِيَامَةِ رَأْيَ عَيْنٍ فَلْيَقْرَأْ: إِذَا الشَّمْسُ كُوِّرَتْ، وَإِذَا السَّمَاءُ انْفَطَرَتْ، وَإِذَا السَّمَاءُ انْشَقَّتْ

"Whoever wishes to look at the Day of Judgement as if he is seeing it with his own eyes, then let him read Sūrah Takweer, Sūrah Infitār and Sūrah Inshiqāq". (Ahmad)

This Sūrah is called Sūrah Takweer or Sūrah Kuwwirat. The above verses describe what will happen on the Day of Judgement. Some of the events described will take place after the first blowing of the trumpet while others will take place after the second blowing of the trumpet.

The following six events will take place after the first blowing of the trumpet:

1)

إِذَا الشَّمْسُ كُوِّرَتْ
'When the sun loses its light'.

Meaning of Takweer

The word Kawwara is derived from Takweer which denotes for the sun to lose its light. Sayyidunā Hasan Basri ﷺ has attached this interpretation to it.

Rabee Ibn Khaitham ﷺ assigns the following interpretation to this verse; The sun will be thrown into the ocean and as a result of its heat, the entire ocean will turn into fire.

The two interpretations are not contradictory. They may be reconciled thus; first, its light will be put off and then it may be thrown into the ocean.

Another meaning of 'Takweer' is to fold. The sense of folding the sun is that its function will come to an end and it will lose its light. As such, it comes to mean the same thing as mentioned in the first interpretation.

Sayyidunā Abū Hurairah ﷺ reports that the Holy Prophet ﷺ said, "On the Day of Judgement, the sun and the moon will be thrown into Hell." (Bukhāri)

In another Hadeeth, it states that on the Day of Judgement, Allāh ﷻ will throw the sun, the moon and the stars into the ocean. Then a violent wind will blow over them, as a result of which the entire ocean will turn into fire.

It is therefore correct to say that the sun and the moon will be put into the ocean. It is likewise correct to say that they will be put into Hell because the entire ocean at that time will have been turned into Hell.

2)

وَإِذَا النُّجُوْمُ انْكَدَرَتْ

When the stars fall down.

The word 'Inkadarat' is derived from 'Inkidār' which means to fall. It signifies that all the stars from the sky will fall into the oceans. In Sūrah Infitār, Allāh ﷻ says,

وَإِذَا الْكَوَاكِبُ انْتَثَرَتْ

When the stars have fallen and scattered (82:2)

Signs of Qiyāmah

Sayyidunā Ubay Ibn Ka'b ؓ states, 'Six Signs will take place before the Day of Judgement. The people will be in their market places when the sun's light will go away. When they are in that situation, the stars will be scattered. When they are in that situation, the mountains will fall down upon the face of the earth, then the earth will move and quake and be in a state of confusion. So the Jinns will then flee in fright to the humans and the humans will flee to the Jinns. The domestic beasts, birds and wild animals will mix together and they will surge together in a wave (of chaos).

11

وَإِذَا الْوُحُوشُ حُشِرَتْ

And when the wild beasts are gathered together.

This means they will all assemble together.

وَإِذَا الْعِشَارُ عُطِّلَتْ

And when the pregnant she-camels are neglected.

This means their owners will neglect them.

وَإِذَا الْبِحَارُ سُجِّرَتْ

And when the seas become a blazing fire.

Then he (Sayyidunā Ubay ﷺ) went on to say, 'The Jinns will say; 'We come to you with news.' So they will all go to the sea and it will be a blazing fire. While they are in that state, the earth will split with one huge crack that will extend from the lowest seventh earth to the highest seventh heaven. While they are in that state, a wind will come that will kill all of them. (Tabarāni)

3)

وَإِذَا الْجِبَالُ سُيِّرَتْ

When the mountains are made to fly about!

The mountains will float in mid-air like the clouds and eventually crumble to dust. Hence, they will not remain in their places and they will be destroyed. Then the earth will be flattened as a levelled plain. How clearly Allāh ﷻ describes the condition of the mountains on that Day.

$$\text{وَيَسْأَلُونَكَ عَنِ الْجِبَالِ فَقُلْ يَنسِفُهَا رَبِّي نَسْفًا . فَيَذَرُهَا قَاعًا صَفْصَفًا . لَا تَرَى فِيهَا عِوَجًا وَّلَا أَمْتًا}$$

"They ask you (O' Rasūlullāh) about the mountains, (What will happen to the mountains on the Day of Judgement?) Say, 'My Lord shall completely remove them (shatter them to dust) leaving the earth as a barren (completely level) plain, on which you will neither see any depressions nor any protrusions (with nothing sunken below or standing above the ground)." (20:105-107)

4)

$$\text{وَإِذَا الْعِشَارُ عُطِّلَتْ}$$
When pregnant camels are forsaken.

The Arabic Word, عِشَارُ 'Ishār' is the plural of the word, عُشَرَا 'Usharā' referring to the she-camel having a ten-month pregnancy. Such she-camels were considered by the Arabs to be a very valuable asset because they expected her to give birth to more camels and produce abundant milk. As such, they used to protect her and never neglect her. The verse referring to this custom of the Arabs, who were the immediate addressee depicts the horrible and terrifying scenes of the Day of Judgement when even the most favourite wealth, like the she-camel, will be abandoned and neglected by its owners because of the calamity they will be facing.

5)

وَإِذَا الْوُحُوشُ حُشِرَتْ

When wild animals are gathered.

Sayyidunā Abdullāh Ibn Abbās ﷺ said: "Everything will be gathered even the flies. Hence, retribution will be taken from every animal that oppressed another in any way. A hornless goat will have revenge from the horned goat that butted it in the world. When revenge is extracted from all the animals, Allāh ﷻ will command them: 'Become dust!'"

The mention of the goat is merely by way of example because the same will apply to all animals. In fact, a Hadeeth reported in Rūhul Ma'āni states that revenge will even be taken from ants. This will of course take place after the second blowing of the trumpet. If this interpretation is applied, it may be said that the verses of the Sūrah merely states the events of Qiyāmat collectively without specifying the sequence.

If we count it within the six events which will take place after the first blowing of the trumpet, then it will be interpreted as when all wild animals will be gathered on the Day of Judgement.

6)

وَإِذَا الْبِحَارُ سُجِّرَتْ

14

When the oceans are set alight.

Sayyidunā Ali ⌐ said to a Jewish man: "Where is Hell?"
The man replied, "The sea."

Sayyidunā Ali ⌐ said, ' I think he is truthful as Allāh ﷻ says,

$$\text{وَالْبَحْرِ الْمَسْجُورِ}$$

"And by the kindled seas." (52:6)

The word 'Sujjirat' is derived from 'Tasjeer' and it signifies 'to set a blaze'. Another meaning of the word is 'to fill' and a third meaning of the word is 'to mix'. None of these meanings are contradictory to each other. First, the salt and sweet water will mix and the rivers shall flow forth into the sea. After that, the seas will meet together becoming one large sea. The seas will then be set on fire and the sun and the moon and the stars will be thrown into the water. Ultimately, all the water will be turned into fire which will become part of Hell.

Thereafter, Allāh ﷻ mentions six events that will take place after the second blowing of the trumpet.

The Six Events

1.

وَإِذَا النُّفُوسُ زُوِّجَتْ

When the souls are joined.

After the disbelievers are separated from the believers, the members of each group will be joined with each other.
Allāh ﷻ says in Sūrah Ibrāheem,

وَتَرَى الْمُجْرِمِينَ يَوْمَئِذٍ مُّقَرَّنِينَ فِي الْأَصْفَادِ

On that Day, you will see the criminals shackled together in chains. (14:49)

In Sūrah Yāseen, Allāh ﷻ says,

وَامْتَازُوا الْيَوْمَ أَيُّهَا الْمُجْرِمُونَ

(The announcement will then be made) 'Separate yourselves (from the believers,) today, O' you criminals (disbelievers).' (36:59)

Hence, on the Day of Judgement, the disbelievers will be grouped with the disbelievers and the believers will be grouped together. There are differences between the deed and habits of believers and there are differences between the deeds and habits of disbelievers. The disbelievers will be regrouped according to their essential characteristics and the believers too will be regrouped according to their essential characteristics.

Sayyidunā Umar Ibn Khattāb ﷺ said that the people doing similar deeds, good or bad will be joined together for example, the knowledgeable people from among the believers, who were serving the Deen will be put into one group, the people who devoted themselves to worship will be made into another group, the people performing Jihād will be together and the people whose main characteristic was to spend in charities will be gathered in one place.

On the other hand, those people who were involved in wicked and evil activities like thieves, robbers, adulterers will also be assembled in their respective groups. Sayyidunā Umar ﷺ based this statement on the verse of the Holy Qur'ān in which Allāh ﷻ says in Sūrah Wāqiyah,

$$\text{وَكُنْتُمْ أَزْوَاجًا ثَلَاثَةً}$$

"And you will be divided into three categories." (56:7)

It is mentioned further in that Sūrah that out of the three categories, two will attain salvation who are named as the Sābiqoon, the foremost and the people of the right while another group, the people of the left will be comprised of the disbelievers.

2.

$$\text{وَإِذَا الْمَوْءُودَةُ سُئِلَتْ . بِأَيِّ ذَنْبٍ قُتِلَتْ}$$

"When the girl buried alive will be asked, 'For what sin was she killed?'"

The polytheists of Arabia during the period of ignorance disliked

17

having daughters and used to bury their infant daughters alive.

Allāh ﷻ says in Sūrah Nahl,

وَإِذَا بُشِّرَ أَحَدُهُمْ بِالْأُنْثَى ظَلَّ وَجْهُهُ مُسْوَدًّا وَهُوَ كَظِيمٌ . يَتَوَارَى مِنَ الْقَوْمِ مِنْ
سُوءِ مَا بُشِّرَ بِهِ أَيُمْسِكُهُ عَلَى هُونٍ أَمْ يَدُسُّهُ فِي التُّرَابِ أَلَا سَاءَ مَا يَحْكُمُونَ

**"When any of them is given the good news of a daughter, his
face darkens and he suppresses his fury. He hides from the people because of the terrible news that he received. Must he keep
her with disgrace or bury her in the sand? Evil indeed is the decision that they make." (16:58-59)**

Islām has abolished this barbaric practice completely. This verse,
whilst describing the scene of the Day of Judgement, mentions that
the girls that were buried alive will be questioned for what crime
they were killed. Apparently, it seems that the question will be
posed to the girl herself. This will give the victim an opportunity to
prove her complete innocence and thus the perpetrators of the
crime will be called up in the divine court of justice and will be du-
ly punished for their wrongdoing.

It is also possible that the question will be posed to the killers of
the girls why they committed infanticide.

A Question

A question may arise here. The Day referred to in these verses is
named as the Day of Judgement and the Day of Reckoning. This

18

name itself shows that every person on that Day will be put to trial where he will be asked all sorts of questions about his deeds. Why has the Holy Qur'ān at this juncture, singled out only the questions asked about the girl who was buried alive. Carefully considered, it would appear that such a girl was the victim of the barbarism of her own parents. As such, there was no one to raise a complaint against such a brutal act, and to demand retaliation, especially when she was buried secretly with no evidence left. The verse therefore signifies that on the Day of Reckoning, even those criminals will be exposed and hauled up in the Divine Court of Justice against whom there was no evidence, nor was there anyone who would stand up on their behalf to demand justice.

Abortion after Four Months (Hundred and Twenty Days)

Burying alive infants or killing them is a major sin and a heinous brutality. Aborting a foetus after four months falls under the same category in the Shariah because upon four months, the foetus receives the soul and hence, treated as a living human being.

When the pregnancy reaches 120 days, an abortion becomes totally forbidden and is tantamount to murder, for it is the taking of an innocent life and killing the baby in the mother's womb. This is the ruling upon which all the Islamic Jurists, past and present have agreed, unanimously condemning such a heinous act.

Note: For a more detailed Fatwa on abortion, refer to 'Ask A Mufti' book.

Abortion before Four Months (Hundred and Twenty Days)

An abortion prior to four months is also unlawful in normal situations according to the majority of scholars but it will not be classified as murder. It will be permitted to have an abortion prior to hundred and twenty days if there is an Islamic valid excuse.

These excuses are of two types:
1)   Those that affect the mother.
2)   Those that affect the unborn child.

Excuses that affect the Mother

- The pregnancy constitutes a danger to the mother's mental health.
- The pregnancy is caused by rape.
- The pregnant woman is severely crippled or suffers from a serious mental illness and is no longer in a position to care for herself, let alone a child, then if it is possible to place the child for adoption after it is born, then an abortion will not be permissible. However, if no such arrangement can be made, it will be permissible to terminate the pregnancy.

Excuses that affect the Unborn Child

- If upon medical examination, it is determined that the child will suffer from severe disabilities or will be inflicted by genetic diseases that will cause the child relentless pain, and that the child will be an undue burden for its parents, then it will be permissible to terminate the pregnancy before four months.

• Pregnancy due to illegitimate sexual intercourse cannot be considered a valid excuse for carrying out an abortion. Islām condemns and rejects illicit sex and everything that may lead to it.

Birth Control

Birth Control and Contraception can be divided into two categories:

1) Irreversible/Permanent Contraception
2) Reversible/Temporary Contraception

Under normal circumstances, irreversible contraception, whether it is in the form of a vasectomy or tubectomy, it is absolutely Harām in Islām.

Islamic laws also prohibits castration. A common factor between castration and a vasectomy is that they both destroy the power of reproduction in a man although the ability to cohabit still exists in both.

Sayyidunā S'ad Ibn Abi Waqqās ؓ relates, "The Messenger of Allāh ﷺ forbade Uthmān Ibn Maz'oon ؓ from abstaining from marriage. If he had allowed him, we would have castrated ourselves." (Bukhāri, Muslim)

21

Sterilisation in dire situations is permitted according to the Jurists. This is based on the guidelines of the Holy Qur'ān and the Hadeeth. In Usūl ul-Fiqh, it is an accepted rule,

اَلضَّرُوْرَاتُ تُبِيْحُ الْمَحْظُوْرَاتِ

'Necessities make prohibitions lawful'.

Hence, if a woman's health or even worse her life is threatened by pregnancy or a woman faces the risk of losing her life after giving birth two or three times through a caesarean operation, and additional births will cause detrimental effects on them, then there is scope of permissibility after seeking professional medical advice from an experienced Muslim doctor.

Reversible Contraception

There are various methods of practicing reversible contraception such as Coitus Interruptus (Azl), the Rhythm Method, Inter-Uterine Devices (IVD), Condoms, Diaphragms and Caps, Oral Contraception Pills, Injections and many more.

Mufti Shafee Sāhib ﷺ says, 'After deducing rulings from the classical books of Hanafi jurisprudence, there are some valid reasons for reversible contraception:

• When a woman is too weak or too ill to sustain the pregnancy.
• When she is in an area where there is no stability or security .
• When the couple are on a prolonged and difficult journey in

which pregnancy may cause difficulty.

- When the wife's relationship with her husband is strained and divorce is likely.

Other scholars have added,

- Spacing out children in order to give them adequate and equal attention.
- When the woman is compelled and forced to seek employment due to unavoidable and desperate circumstances.

We need to remember that practicing contraception for fear of poverty or contraception out of shame of conceiving a girl or for the fashion of having small families will not be permissible.

Book of Deeds

3)

وَإِذَا الصُّحُفُ نُشِرَتْ

When the records of deeds will be opened.

Every person will receive his record of deeds on the Day of Judgement. The successful ones will receive theirs in their right hands while the unsuccessful ones will receive theirs in their left hands.

Allāh ﷻ says in Sūrah Banū Isrāeel,

وَنُخْرِجُ لَهُ يَوْمَ الْقِيَامَةِ كِتَابًا يَّلْقَاهُ مَنْشُوْرًا . اِقْرَأْ كِتَابَكَ كَفَى بِنَفْسِكَ الْيَوْمَ عَلَيْكَ حَسِيْبًا

23

'On the Day of Judgement, We shall take out for him a book that
he will see opened before him. Read your book. Today you are a
sufficient witness against yourself.' (17:13-14)

Allāh ﷻ says in Sūrah Kahf,

وَوُضِعَ الْكِتَابُ فَتَرَى الْمُجْرِمِينَ مُشْفِقِينَ مِمَّا فِيهِ وَيَقُولُونَ يَا وَيْلَتَنَا مَالِ هٰذَا الْكِتَابِ لَا
يُغَادِرُ صَغِيرَةً وَّلَا كَبِيرَةً إِلَّا أَحْصَاهَا وَوَجَدُوا مَا عَمِلُوا حَاضِرًا وَلَا يَظْلِمُ رَبُّكَ أَحَدًا

'The record of deeds shall be placed and you will see the sinners
afraid of what is contained in them. They will say: 'Woe to us!
What is with this book that it does not leave anything small or
large unrecorded? They will find their deeds present and your
Lord shall not oppress anyone.' (18:49)

4)

وَإِذَا السَّمَاءُ كُشِطَتْ

When the sky will be opened

The word 'Kushitat' is derived from 'Kasht', and it literally means
to strip off the skin of an animal. Probably, this condition will prevail in the first blowing of the trumpet, which will happen in this
world. The stars, the sun and the moon that contributed to the
beauty of the sky will all lose their light and lustre and will be
thrown into the oceans. The outlook of the sky will be changed.

5)

وَإِذَا الْجَحِيمُ سُعِّرَتْ

When Jahannam will 'be fuelled' (to make it burn more intensely)

6)

وَإِذَا الْجَنَّةُ أُزْلِفَتْ

When Jannah will be brought close.

Jannah will be brought close to the pious whereas Jahannam will be brought close to the disbelievers, as Allāh ﷻ says in Sūrah Shu'arā,

وَأُزْلِفَتِ الْجَنَّةُ لِلْمُتَّقِينَ . وَبُرِّزَتِ الْجَحِيمُ لِلْغَاوِينَ

"Jannah will be brought close to the pious while Jahannam will be revealed to the deviant ones." (26:90-91)

When all these events will take place, on that Day every soul will know what (deeds) it has presented. People will then realise whether they are destined for Jannah or Jahannam.
Allāh ﷻ says,

يَوْمَ تَجِدُ كُلُّ نَفْسٍ مَّا عَمِلَتْ مِنْ خَيْرٍ مُّحْضَرًا وَّمَا عَمِلَتْ مِنْ سُوءٍ تَوَدُّ لَوْ أَنَّ بَيْنَهَا وَبَيْنَهُ أَمَدًا بَعِيدًا

"On the Day when every person will be confronted with all the good he has done and all the evil he has done, he will wish that there was a great distance between him and his evil." (3:30)

25

In another verse, Allāh ﷻ says,

يُنَبَّأُ الْإِنْسَانُ يَوْمَئِذٍ بِمَا قَدَّمَ وَأَخَّرَ

**"On that Day, man will be informed of what he sent forward
and what he left behind." (75:13)**

فَلَا أُقْسِمُ بِالْخُنَّسِ . الْجَوَارِ الْكُنَّسِ . وَاللَّيْلِ إِذَا عَسْعَسَ . وَالصُّبْحِ إِذَا تَنَفَّسَ . إِنَّهُ لَقَوْلُ رَسُولٍ كَرِيمٍ . ذِي قُوَّةٍ عِنْدَ ذِي الْعَرْشِ مَكِينٍ . مُّطَاعٍ ثَمَّ أَمِينٍ . وَمَا صَاحِبُكُمْ بِمَجْنُونٍ . وَلَقَدْ رَآهُ بِالْأُفُقِ الْمُبِينِ . وَمَا هُوَ عَلَى الْغَيْبِ بِضَنِينٍ . وَمَا هُوَ بِقَوْلِ شَيْطَانٍ رَّجِيمٍ . فَأَيْنَ تَذْهَبُونَ . إِنْ هُوَ إِلَّا ذِكْرٌ لِّلْعَالَمِينَ . لِمَنْ شَاءَ مِنْكُمْ أَنْ يَسْتَقِيمَ . وَمَا تَشَاءُونَ إِلَّا أَنْ يَشَاءَ اللهُ رَبُّ الْعَالَمِينَ

15. I swear by the planets that recede.
16. That travel and hide.
17. And (I swear by) the night when it departs.
18. And by the morning when it takes a breath.
19. Undoubtedly, this Qur'ān is a word brought by an honoured Messenger (Sayyidunā Jibreel)
20. Who is powerful and of high rank in the sight of the Owner of the Throne.
21. He is also obeyed there and is trustworthy.
22. Verily your Companion is not insane.
23. He certainly saw him on the clear horizon.
24. He is also not miserly with the knowledge of the unseen.
25. The Holy Qur'ān is not the word of any accursed Shaytān.

26. So where are you heading?
27. It is but a great advice to the universe.
28. For those of you who take the straight path.
29. You cannot will anything without the will of Allāh, the Lord of the Universe.

The Holy Qur'ān

Allāh ﷻ takes several oaths in this Sūrah to assert the fact that, **"Undoubtedly this Qur'ān is a word brought by an honoured Messenger (Sayyidunā Jibreel)."**

These verses also refute the statement of those disbelievers who claimed that the Holy Prophet ﷺ was insane.

Allāh ﷻ says,

$$\text{فَلَا أُقْسِمُ بِالْخُنَّسِ . الْجَوَارِ الْكُنَّسِ}$$

"I swear by the planets that recede, that travel and hide."

Sayyidunā Ali ؓ has mentioned that the planets referred to in these verses are Saturn, Mercury, Jupiter, Mars and Venus. These verses refer to the rising and setting of the planets which appear like stars in the sky, and the verses make it clear that they travel on their orbits as well.

$$\text{وَاللَّيْلِ إِذَا عَسْعَسَ}$$

"And I swear by the night when it departs."

Some commentators translate this verse as, **"By the night when it brings darkness."** They say that this interpretation is more appropriate because it refers to the beginning of the night, and the next verse,

$$\text{وَالصُّبْحِ إِذَا تَنَفَّسَ}$$

"By the morning when it takes a breath"

refers to the closing of the night i.e. the arrival of the day. In this way, both parts of the night are referred to.

The word 'As'as' has both meanings 'Idbār' (to leave) and 'Iqbāl,' (to approach). Both meanings could be referred to at this juncture.

Angel Jibreel ﷺ

Allāh ﷻ then swears the oath to assert,

$$\text{إِنَّه لَقَوْلُ رَسُولٍ كَرِيْمٍ . ذِي قُوَّةٍ عِنْدَ ذِي الْعَرْشِ مَكِيْنٍ . مُّطَاعٍ ثَمَّ أَمِيْنٍ}$$

"Undoubtedly this Holy Qur'ān is a word brought by an honoured Messenger (Sayyidunā Jibreel) who is powerful and of
high rank in the sight of the Owner of the Throne. He is also
obeyed there (in the heavens) and trustworthy."

The fact that Allāh ﷻ entrusted Sayyidunā Jibreel ﷺ to convey
revelation to the Prophets ﷺ proves that he must certainly be
trustworthy. In these verses, three qualities are attributed to this
noble Messenger; the first quality is demonstrated numerous times
when he was assigned by Allāh ﷻ to destroy certain nations e.g.
the nation of Loot. Allāh ﷻ says,

$$\text{عَلَّمَه شَدِيْدُ الْقُوٰى}$$

"He is taught by the one of tremendous might." (53:5)

The second quality is that he has high status and lofty rank with
Allāh ﷻ and he is obeyed in the upper realm. He is not one from
the lower ranking ordinary angels, he is respected and has been
chosen for (the delivery of) this magnificent message. The third
quality is that he is trusted and there is no possibility of him per-
petrating any breach of trust or tampering with the message he
conveys.

29

The Holy Prophet ﷺ

وَمَا صَاحِبُكُم بِمَجْنُونٍ

"Verily your Companion is not insane."

After mentioning about Sayyidunā Jibreel ﷺ, Allāh ﷻ speaks of the Holy Prophet ﷺ. Allāh ﷻ says, **"Verily your Companion is not insane."** The polytheists of Makkah knew the Holy Prophet ﷺ very well and they were convinced that none could be more truthful and honest than the Holy Prophet ﷺ.

When Allāh ﷻ chooses a certain individual for a divine task, then He very well knows who qualifies for that position. He says,

اللهُ أَعْلَمُ حَيْثُ يَجْعَلُ رِسَالَتَه

"Allāh knows best where He wishes to place this message." (6:124)

When the polytheists of Makkah instead of accepting the Holy Qur'ān said,

وَقَالُوا لَوْلَا نُزِّلَ هَذَا الْقُرْآنُ عَلَى رَجُلٍ مِّنَ الْقَرْيَتَيْنِ عَظِيمٍ

"Why is this Qur'ān not revealed to a prominent man from one of the two cities (Makkah or Tā'if, instead of being revealed to the Holy Prophet?) (43:31)

Allāh ﷻ immediately answers them,

$$أَهُمۡ يَقۡسِمُونَ رَحۡمَةَ رَبِّكَ$$

"Do they distribute (allocate) the mercy (prophethood) of your Lord?" (43:32)

Obviously they have no choice in selecting who Allāh's ﷻ Messenger should be. Even in regards to worldly matters, He says,

$$نَحۡنُ قَسَمۡنَا بَيۡنَهُم مَّعِيشَتَهُمۡ فِي الۡحَيَاةِ الدُّنۡيَا وَرَفَعۡنَا بَعۡضَهُمۡ فَوۡقَ بَعۡضٍ دَرَجَاتٍ لِّيَتَّخِذَ بَعۡضُهُم بَعۡضًا سُخۡرِيًّا وَرَحۡمَتُ رَبِّكَ خَيۡرٌ مِّمَّا يَجۡمَعُونَ$$

"We distribute their livelihood among them in this worldly life and (thereby) elevate the ranks of some of them above others so that they may derive benefit from each other (by being inter dependent). (When this is the state of affairs concerning worldly matters) the mercy of your Lord (prophethood which is related to the Hereafter) is better than what (wealth) they amass." (43:32)

It is therefore Allāh's ﷻ right to decide who receives the mantle of prophethood.

Hakeemul Ummah Shaykh Ashraf Ali Thānwi ﷫ says, "The oaths of Allāh ﷻ in these verses are extremely apt, while the travelling and hiding of the planets symbolise the travelling of the Angels and their disappearance into the heavens, the departure of the night and arrival of the day symbolise the departure of Kufr (disbelief) and arrival of Imān (the light)- the cause of this being

31

the Holy Qur'ān and the Holy Prophet ﷺ.

The Holy Prophet ﷺ certainly saw Sayyidunā Jibreel عليه السلام on the clear horizon. Sayyidunā Jibreel عليه السلام normally met the Holy Prophet ﷺ in the appearance of a Sahābi by the name of Sayyidunā Dihya Kalbi ﵁. However, the Holy Prophet ﷺ saw him twice in his original form. In this verse, it refers to the first sighting which occurred in Makkah, Allāh ﷻ mentions this incident in Sūrah Najm.

"He has been taught by one of tremendous might (Sayyidunā Jibreel) and who is extremely powerful (so powerful that he used only the tip of one of his 600 wings to lift the city of Sodom). Sayyidunā Jibreel usually appeared before the Holy Prophet in human form. He (Sayyidunā Jibreel) once appeared (before the Holy Prophet) in his original form (in Makkah). When he (Sayyidunā Jibreel) was on the highest part of the horizon, the Holy Prophet saw Sayyidunā Jibreel on the Eastern horizon with his six hundred wings spread out. They were so large that they even covered the Western horizon. The sight was so tremendous that the Holy Prophet fell unconscious. Then, (seeing the Holy Prophet fall unconscious) he (Sayyidunā Jibreel approached the Holy Prophet to revive him) and (doing this, he) drew close and was as close (to the Holy Prophet) as two bows (with each end of a bow touching the **corresponding end of the other bow) or even closer. Then Allāh sent that revelation to His slave which He revealed." (53:5-10)**

The second sighting has been mentioned further in the Sūrah,

"He (the Holy Prophet) certainly saw him (Sayyidunā Jibreel) in his original form once more (a second time) at the Sidratul Muntahā (near the Lote tree when the Holy Prophet went on the miraculous journey of Mi'rāj to the furthest Jannah) close to which is Jannatul Ma'wā (a comfortable dwelling above which is Allāh's throne)." (53:13-15)

Miraculous Qur'ān

Allāh ﷻ continues to say that the Holy Prophet ﷺ is not miserly with the knowledge of the unseen i.e. he conveys all the revelation that he is responsible to convey.

The disbelievers threw all types of allegations upon the Holy Prophet ﷺ regarding the revelation which Allāh ﷻ answers in different places of the Holy Qur'ān.

In Sūrah Hāqqah, Allāh ﷻ after swearing an oath by things that you see and by the things that you do not see, He says,

"Verily this Qur'ān is brought to the Holy Prophet by an honoured Messenger (Sayyidunā Jibreel), it is not the speech of a poet, (however, despite the proofs) few are those (of you) who have Imān. Neither is it the speech of a fortune teller. (Despite knowing this) few are those (of you) who understand (who will ponder). It is a revelation from the Lord of the Universe." (69:40-43)

Allāh ﷻ further says,

"The Qur'ān is not the word of any accursed Shaytān. So where are you heading?"

Once it has been established that the Messenger, Angel Jibreel عليه السلام has all the right credentials and the Messenger Muhammad ﷺ is also truthful beyond doubt, how can one wander astray thinking that the Holy Qur'ān is doubtful.

In Sūrah Shu'arā, Allāh ﷻ says,

وَمَا تَنَزَّلَتْ بِهِ الشَّيَاطِينُ . وَمَا يَنْبَغِي لَهُمْ وَمَا يَسْتَطِيعُونَ . إِنَّهُمْ عَنِ السَّمْعِ لَمَعْزُولُونَ

"The Shayāteen have not brought it (the Qur'ān) down. It (bringing down the Qur'ān) is not suited to them (because while the Qur'ān provides guidance, the Shayāteen can provide only misguidance), nor have they the capability (to overhear any part of the Qur'ān in the heavens, before it was transmitted to the Holy Prophet because Allāh had sealed off the corridors to the heavens for them, and whoever tried to overhear something was destroyed by a flaming star). They (the Shayāteen) have definitely been forbidden from listening (to the revelation of the Qur'ān in the heavens)." (26: 210-212)

How compassionately Allāh ﷻ addresses mankind by proclaiming, "O my beloved servants! Where are you going?" Meaning, where has your reason gone in rejecting this Holy Qur'ān, while it is manifest, clear and evident that it is the truth from Allāh ﷻ, so come back to me. Allāhu Akbar!

34

In the caliphate of Sayyidunā Abū Bakr Siddeeq ◌, a delegation of
Banū Haneefah came to Madeenah Munawwarah, so he (Abū Bakr
◌) commanded them to recite (something from the Qur'ān), so
they recited something to him from the so called Qur'ān of Musail-
amah, the liar that was total gibberish and terribly poor in style.
Thus, Sayyidunā Abū Bakr ◌ said, "Woe unto you (where have
your senses gone? By Allāh ◌, this speech did not come from
Allāh ◌."

Allāh ◌ after consolidating the authority of the Holy Qur'ān that,
it is not the word of a Shaytān, or a soothsayer, or a madman, or a
poet, or a person who has ulterior motives, he proclaims that the
Holy Qur'ān is a great advice to the universe, for those of you who
wish to tread the straight path.

When the verse, **"For those of you who wish to tread the straight
path"** was revealed, Abū Jahl said, "The matter is up to us. If we
wish, we will stand straight and if we do not wish, we will not
stand straight." So Allāh ◌ revealed, **"(However) you cannot will
anything without the will of Allāh, the Lord of the universe."**
Everything is in Allāh's ◌ control, even guidance.

Allāh ◌ addresses the Holy Prophet ◌ when he became so grieved
that he was unable to get his uncle Abū Tālib to accept Islām before he died,

إِنَّكَ لَا تَهْدِيْ مَنْ أَحْبَبْتَ وَلٰكِنَّ اللهَ يَهْدِيْ مَنْ يَّشَاءُ وَهُوَ أَعْلَمُ بِالْمُهْتَدِيْنَ

"Verily you (O' Holy Prophet) cannot guide those whom you

love (to Islām), but Allāh guides whoever He wills. He is best aware of those who are (deserving to be) rightly guided (and who deserve to be guided to Imān)." (28:56)

In another verse, He clearly says,

وَمَا كَانَ لِنَفْسٍ أَن تُؤْمِنَ إِلَّا بِإِذْنِ اللّهِ

"No soul can have Imān without Allāh's order (will and grace)." (10:100)

May Allāh ﷻ keep us steadfast on our Imān till our last breath. May He keep us punctual in His obedience and give us death upon Imān. Āmeen.

Sūrah Infitār

The Splitting
Revealed in Makkah

بِسْمِ اللهِ الرَّحْمٰنِ الرَّحِيْمِ

In the Name of Allāh, the Most Compassionate, the Most Merciful

إِذَا السَّمَاءُ انْفَطَرَتْ . وَإِذَا الْكَوَاكِبُ انْتَثَرَتْ . وَإِذَا الْبِحَارُ فُجِّرَتْ . وَإِذَا الْقُبُوْرُ بُعْثِرَتْ . عَلِمَتْ نَفْسٌ مَّا قَدَّمَتْ وَأَخَّرَتْ

1. When the sky splits.
2. When the stars will disperse.
3. When the seas will burst forth.
4. And when the graves are overturned.
5. Every soul shall come to know what it had sent ahead and left behind.

Virtues of Sūrah Infitār

Imām Nasai 🙵 reports from Sayyidunā Jābir 🙵 that Sayyidunā Muādh 🙵 stood and lead the people in the Ishā Salāh and he made the recitation of his prayer long, so the Holy Prophet 🙵 said,

أَفَتَّانٌ أَنْتَ يَامُعَاذُ , أَيْنَ كُنْتَ عَنْ سَبِّحِ اسْمَ رَبِّكَ الْأَعْلَى والضُّحٰى وإِذَا السَّمَاءُ انْفَطَرَتْ

"Are you putting the people to trial, O' Muādh? Why don't you recite Sūrah A'lā, Sūrah Duhā and Sūrah Infitār?"

In the opening verses of Sūrah Takweer, the Hadeeth of Sayyidunā Abdullāh Ibn Umar ؓ has been mentioned where the Holy Prophet ﷺ said,

مَنْ سَرَّهُ أَنْ يَّنْظُرَ إِلَى الْقِيَامَةِ رَأْىَ عَيْنٍ فَلْيَقْرَأْ: إِذَا الشَّمْسُ كُوِّرَتْ، وَإِذَا السَّمَاءُ انْفَطَرَتْ، وَإِذَا السَّمَاءُ انْشَقَّتْ

"Whoever wishes to look at the Day of Resurrection as if he is seeing it with his own eyes, then let him recite Sūrah Takweer, Sūrah Infitār and Sūrah Inshiqāq." (Ahmad)

The opening verses of Sūrah Infitār draws the picture of the Day of Judgement similar to what was mentioned in the opening verses of Sūrah Takweer in the previous Sūrah. These two Sūrahs i.e. Sūrah Takweer and Sūrah Infitār have so many similarities. They both discuss the severity of the Judgement Day, they both remind mankind of his pitiful plight on the Day of Resurrection, they both prewarn the grave consequences of denying Allāh ﷻ. It has been said that these two Sūrahs are so bonded together that it is as though it has one heart with two bodies.

The first three verses, **"When the sky splits, the stars fall, the oceans are poured forth (i.e. fresh and salt water bodies will merge to become one mass of water)"** are referring to those occurrences that will take place after the first blowing of the trumpet.

Preparation for the Hereafter

The fourth verse is referring to the graves and when the graves are overturned and emptied together with their contents so that people appear before Allāh ﷻ for reckoning. This will take place after the second blowing of the trumpet.

$$\text{عَلِمَتْ نَفْسٌ مَّا قَدَّمَتْ وَأَخَّرَتْ}$$

"Every soul shall come to know what it had sent ahead and left behind."

The phrase 'what it had sent ahead' means the good or evil act which he has done in his life and the phrase, 'what it has left behind' means what he failed to do or refrained from doing. It also can refer to the actions that he has done himself and 'what he left behind' refers to the actions one has not done himself, but he has laid down a good practice in the society.

In a Hadeeth of Muslim, narrated by Sayyidunā Abū Mas'ood Ansāri ؓ, it states,

$$\text{مَنْ دَلَّ عَلَى خَيْرٍ فَلَهُ مِثْلُ أَجْرِ فَاعِلِه}$$

"For him who directs towards good has the same reward as the doer" (Muslim)

In a Hadeeth of Mishkāt, it states, "If anyone initiates a good practice in Islām, he will have a reward for it and the equivalent of the reward of those who act upon it after him, without their reward decreasing in any amount, but the one who initiates a bad practice (or custom) in Islām will bear the responsibility (sin) of it and the burden (sin) of those who practice upon it after him without their sin being reduced in any respect."

Therefore, whoever directs people towards good deeds either through speech, teaching, action or writing, will in return receive immense reward. In a Hadeeth of Ibn Mājah, the Holy Prophet ﷺ outlined some of the deeds which will reach the believer after his death.

إِنَّ مِمَّا يَلْحَقُ الْمُؤْمِنَ مِنْ عَمَلِهِ وَحَسَنَاتِهِ بَعْدَ مَوْتِهِ عِلْمًا عَلَّمَهُ وَنَشَرَهُ ، أَوْ وَلَدًا صَالِحًا تَرَكَهُ ، أَوْ مُصْحَفًا وَرَّثَهُ ، أَوْ مَسْجِدًا بَنَاهُ ، أَوْ بَيْتًا لِابْنِ السَّبِيْلِ بَنَاهُ ، أَوْ نَهْرًا أَجْرَاهُ ، أَوْ صَدَقَةً أَخْرَجَهَا مِنْ مَالِهِ فِيْ صِحَّتِهِ وَحَيَاتِهِ تَلْحَقُهُ مِنْ بَعْدِ مَوْتِهِ

"Among those actions and good deeds (whose reward) a believer will recover after his death are, sacred knowledge he taught and spread, a pious child he left behind, a copy of the Holy Qur'ān he left as a legacy, a Masjid he constructed, or a home he built for the traveller, or a stream he set flowing, or voluntary charity he gave from his wealth while he was alive and healthy. They will continue to reach him after his death." (Ibn Mājah)

يَا أَيُّهَا الْإِنْسَانُ مَا غَرَّكَ بِرَبِّكَ الْكَرِيْمِ . الَّذِيْ خَلَقَكَ فَسَوَّاكَ فَعَدَلَكَ . فِيْ أَيِّ صُوْرَةٍ مَّا شَاءَ رَكَّبَكَ

6. **O' Mankind! What has cast you into deception concerning your Most Generous Lord.**

40

7. Who has created you, perfected you, gave you due proportion.
8. And made you into the fashion He desired.

Man - The Best of Creation

Describing the creation of man, Allāh ﷻ reminds man to turn attention towards Him. Man was absolutely nothing when Allāh ﷻ created him, perfected his form and according to His perfect wisdom, made him as He pleased. Neither did man have the option to be created nor did he have a choice to decide his height, size or features. Every person is as Allāh ﷻ made him and lives in this condition. It is now compulsory on every individual to accept the commands of Allāh ﷻ that His Messengers brought forth to them.

There have always been two groups amongst people. One group, the Hizbullāh – the group who have accepted the Deen of Allāh ﷻ and the Hizbush-Shaytān – those who have rejected.

From amongst those who have accepted the Deen of Allāh ﷻ are those who neglect His command, and continue sinning. When it is brought to their attention, that this type of life is incorrect, their Nafs and Shaytān fool them into thinking that there is no need to curb their ways because Allāh ﷻ is Most Generous and Kind and will continue forgiving them. They fail to realise that because Allāh ﷻ is so Magnanimous and Gracious, He deserves to be obeyed.

The weakness of man is that he has no sense of loyalty and is not faithful to Allāh ﷻ. Despite the innumerable bounties and favours

41

that Allāh ﷻ bestows upon man, man still disobeys Him. Even if it was certain that every sin will be forgiven without punishment, it would be compulsory upon mankind to obey Allāh's ﷻ command. Obeying Allāh's ﷻ commands merely because one fears punishment, is a sign of disloyalty. A loyal servant shivers at the mere thought of disobeying Allāh ﷻ. Such a servant looks at the great bounties that Allāh ﷻ blesses him with and without concentrating only on the punishment for disobedience, he engages himself in fulfilling the commands at hand. In fact, he regards leading a life of disobedience as a punishment of its own.

Although punishment causes physical pain, the pain that the faithful servant feels at the time of disloyalty is greater than the pain of any punishment.

Restraining the Nafs

How beautifully our beloved Prophet ﷺ said,

اَلْكَيِّسُ مَنْ دَانَ نَفْسَه وَعَمِلَ لِمَا بَعْدَ الْمَوْتِ، وَالْعَاجِزُ مَنْ أَتْبَعَ نَفْسَه هَوَاهَا وَتَمَنَّى عَلَى اللهِ

The intelligent one is he who has subdued his lower-self and who has worked for what comes after death, and the fool is he who has put his lower-self in pursuance of its desires and who has vain hopes about Allāh ﷻ. (Tirmizi, Ibn Mājah)

That person who subdues his lower self is that person who renders himself in complete obedience to the commands of Allāh ﷻ. In this parable, the one who carries vain hopes about Allāh ﷻ is the one who thinks, **"My Lord is Most Generous and Most Merciful"** and forgets that Allāh ﷻ has not only said,

$$ يَاأَيُّهَا الْإِنْسَانُ مَا غَرَّكَ بِرَبِّكَ الْكَرِيْمِ $$

"O' man! What has deceived you from your Lord, Most Beneficent." (82:6)

but He has also announced,

$$ نَبِّئْ عِبَادِيْ أَنِّيْ أَنَا الْغَفُوْرُ الرَّحِيْمُ . وَأَنَّ عَذَابِيْ هُوَ الْعَذَابُ الْأَلِيْمُ $$

"Tell My servants that I am indeed the Oft-Forgiving, Most Merciful and that My Punishment will be indeed the most grievous punishment." (15:49-50)

Allāh's ﷻ Compassion

The opening verses of this Sūrah mentions the horrific events that will take place at the extinction of every living thing, and the current set of verses remind us of the initial stages of our creation. The conclusion of the verses is that if man had considered carefully and pondered over his condition, he would have surely believed in Allāh ﷻ and His Messenger ﷺ and would not have deviated an inch from the commandments of Allāh ﷻ.

In the present verse, he is reprimanded by a rhetorical question and by means of gentle reproach as to what has lured him away from His Gracious Lord and led him to disobedience, despite knowing the beginning and the ending of his life. Subhān'Allāh.

43

In Tafseer Ibn Katheer, it mentions that Allāh will say on the Day of Judgement, **"O' Son of Ādam! What has deceived you concerning Me? O' Son of Ādam! What was your response to the Messenger?"**

Imām Baghawi mentions that Kalbi and Muqātil said, "This verse was revealed about Aswad Ibn Shareeq who struck the Holy Prophet and he was not punished in retaliation, so Allāh revealed,

مَا غَرَّكَ بِرَبِّكَ الْكَرِيمِ

"What has deceived you from your Lord, Most Beneficent." (82:6)

How compassionate Allāh is, He reminds man again and again about his origin so that he does not forget it and become ungrateful.

But alas! He is so heedless. Allāh says, **"He Who has created you, perfected (shaped) you, gave you (your body) due proportion and made you in the fashion He desired (without making you into something despicable)."**

Allāh did not only create man but He also perfected his creation and proportioned his body, limbs and organs. Every limb and organ is well placed. The body, height, length and breadth of every limbs are kept in harmony, symmetry and balance. Any deviation from the symmetrical construction of the human body, will make the organs dysfunctional. Then the verse says,

44

فَعَدَلَكَ

"Then brought you into due proportion." (82:7)

Man is granted such symmetry, harmony and balance that no other animal in the world is granted to that degree. Along with physical and physiological symmetry, he has been granted well-balanced disposition - despite the fact that man is made up of opposing humours – some hot and others are cold and yet the perfect wisdom of Allāh ﷺ prepared a well-balanced disposition.

Thereafter, a third characteristic is mentioned as follows,

فِىٓ أَىِّ صُورَةٍ مَّا شَآءَ رَكَّبَكَ

"He made you in the fashion He desired." (82:8)

This is to indicate that since the basic structure of all human beings is the same, it was expected that the trillions of members of the human society would have shared the same shape, size and features but Allāhu Akbar - the perfect mastery and the wonderful acumen of the Supreme Creator has created them so differently that each one of them has its own unique features that make him clearly distinct from all others, and no one is confused with one another.

How wonderfully Allāh ﷺ says,

سَنُرِيهِمْ آيَاتِنَا فِي الْآفَاقِ وَفِي أَنْفُسِهِمْ حَتَّى يَتَبَيَّنَ لَهُمْ أَنَّهُ الْحَقُّ أَوَلَمْ يَكْفِ بِرَبِّكَ أَنَّهُ عَلَى كُلِّ شَيْءٍ شَهِيدٌ

45

"(Nevertheless) We shall soon show them Our signs on the horizons (of the world) and within themselves, until it becomes clear to them that it (the Holy Qur'ān) is certainly the truth. Is it not sufficient that your Lord is Witness over everything? (41:53)

Hence, if we ponder over our creation, we will concede and confirm the truth without a shadow of doubt.

كَلَّا بَلْ تُكَذِّبُوْنَ بِالدِّيْنِ . وَإِنَّ عَلَيْكُمْ لَحَافِظِيْنَ . كِرَامًا كَاتِبِيْنَ . يَعْلَمُوْنَ مَا تَفْعَلُوْنَ . إِنَّ الْأَبْرَارَ لَفِيْ نَعِيْمٍ . وَإِنَّ الْفُجَّارَ لَفِيْ جَحِيْمٍ . يَصْلَوْنَهَا يَوْمَ الدِّيْنِ . وَمَا هُمْ عَنْهَا بِغَائِبِيْنَ . وَمَا أَدْرَاكَ مَا يَوْمُ الدِّيْنِ . ثُمَّ مَا أَدْرَاكَ مَا يَوْمُ الدِّيْنِ . يَوْمَ لَا تَمْلِكُ نَفْسٌ لِّنَفْسٍ شَيْئًا وَالْأَمْرُ يَوْمَئِذٍ لِّلّٰهِ

9. It should never be! The fact is that they deny retribution.
10. Verily there are guardians upon you.
11. Who are noble and are recording.
12. They know what you do.
13. Indeed the righteous shall be immersed in bounties.
14. And the sinners will surely be in Jahannam.
15. Which they will enter on the Day of Retribution.
16. They will certainly not be absent from it.
17. Do you know what the Day of Retribution is?
18. Do you really know what the Day of Retribution is?
19. It shall be a Day when one soul will be unable to benefit another soul in the least. On that Day, all authority will be Allāh's.

Kirāman Kātibeen

Allāh ﷻ says, **"It should never be!"** i.e. one should never be deceived by his Nafs and by Shaytān. By being deceived, one will harm only oneself.

The result of this is that people will deny that retribution will take place and they will become reckless in their behaviour. For this reason, Allāh ﷻ reminds them,

"Verily there are guardians upon you who are noble (in Allāh's sight) and are recording. They know what you do."

It is therefore best for people to carry out good deeds and to refrain from sins. The guardian angels, whom Allāh ﷻ has assigned with every person preserve and document every act which is carried out by the individual.

Allāh ﷻ says,

"(Do not forget each time) When two receivers (angels) receive (record the good and bad acts of a person), sitting on his right and left hand sides (respectively). Whenever a word escapes (from a person's mouth), there is a guard ready by him. (An angel immediately records the good or bad speech)."

These angels have the quality and attribute of كَرَمٌ (kindness) in them like Allāh ﷻ.

i.e.   بِرَبِّكَ الْكَرِيْم

47

What is the kindness and generosity they display towards men?

Firstly, the angels remain hidden from man. They do not present themselves in a visible form lest man becomes embarrassed to become intimate with his spouse or in relieving himself at the call of nature.

Secondly, it is their benevolence and kindness that they do not disgrace and humiliate man even though they know every act of his. They do not disclose any of his secrets to anyone.

Thirdly, from their kindness is that when one carries out one good deed, they multiply and write it as ten good deeds. Hence, if a person gives one pound in the path of Allāh 🕮, he will receive as though he has given ten pounds and this is just the starting point, the minimum amount. According to a person's sincerity and other factors, it has the potential to increase manifold to thousands as mentioned in the Holy Qur'ān and Ahādeeth. Similarly, if a person intended to carry out a good deed and for whatever reason he could not perform this deed, then they will write this as if one good deed was performed. Likewise, a person made an intention to commit a sin but did not, so the noble angels will write it as a good deed performed.

Furthermore, if a person commits a sin, the angels do not immediately write that sin but wait anxiously for some hours and give man respite to either repent sincerely or carry out some good deeds which will wipe out the sin committed. Even then, if a person did not repent or carry out a good deed – only one sin is

written which will be pending upon Tawbah (repentance) and forgiveness, or carrying out a good deed. If any of these acts are carried out then the sin is erased from the record books.

Subhān'Allāh!

These noble angels even though they are very meticulous in their
memory and retaining power, they write every single act or word
uttered by man, so no one can deny them. Allāh ﷻ says, **"They
know what you do"** i.e. nothing is hidden from them. According
to the Ahādeeth, there are four Kirāman Kātibeen angels – two are
assigned for the day shift and two for the night shift. They have
their own separate registers – one for day time and one for night
time – each one leaves the register for their colleague when their
shift ends.

There is a difference of opinion within the scholars regarding these
angels as to whether they know the intentions hidden in the heart
or not. From the previous verses quoted, it seems that they only
know those matters which men express verbally or by actions.
They do not know what is in the hearts – which only Allāh ﷻ has
the knowledge about. But at the same time, the famous Hadeeth
where it mentions about the intention – if it is good then one deed
is written and if it is bad – and he doesn't carry it out then one
good deed is written – that demonstrates that they have the
knowledge of the hidden thoughts. Those who differ in this point
argue that this matter is inspired to them by Allāh ﷻ that My certain servant has made these certain intentions, so write them
down. This view seems more acceptable. Only Allāh ﷻ knows
best!

Abode of the Righteous and Sinners

Indeed, the righteous shall be immersed in bounties – those who made their preparations properly and preserved their good deeds beforehand from this world. It will then be said to them, "Eat and drink coupled with all the blessings as a reward for the (good) deeds that you sent ahead during the days gone by (in this world).

The sinners will surely be in Jahannam which they will enter on the Day of Retribution. They will certainly not be absent from it. They will have to suffer eternally in Jahannam and will be unable to escape. Allāh ﷻ refers to the same in Sūrah Mā'idah when He says,

$$\text{وَمَا هُم بِخَارِجِينَ مِنْهَا وَلَهُمْ عَذَابٌ مُّقِيمٌ}$$

"They will try to escape and for them there will be a permanent chastisement." (5:37)

Allāh ﷻ mentions the plight of the sinners in Sūrah Hāqqah,

$$\text{وَأَمَّا مَنْ أُوتِيَ كِتَابَهُ بِشِمَالِهِ فَيَقُولُ يَا لَيْتَنِي لَمْ أُوتَ كِتَابِيَهْ . وَلَمْ أَدْرِ مَا حِسَابِيَهْ .}$$
$$\text{يَا لَيْتَهَا كَانَتِ الْقَاضِيَةَ . مَا أَغْنَى عَنِّي مَالِيَهْ . هَلَكَ عَنِّي سُلْطَانِيَهْ . خُذُوهُ فَغُلُّوهُ . ثُمَّ}$$
$$\text{الْجَحِيمَ صَلُّوهُ . ثُمَّ فِي سِلْسِلَةٍ ذَرْعُهَا سَبْعُونَ ذِرَاعًا فَاسْلُكُوهُ . إِنَّهُ كَانَ لَا يُؤْمِنُ بِاللهِ}$$
$$\text{الْعَظِيمِ . وَلَا يَحُضُّ عَلَى طَعَامِ الْمِسْكِينِ . فَلَيْسَ لَهُ الْيَوْمَ هَاهُنَا حَمِيمٌ . وَلَا طَعَامٌ}$$
$$\text{إِلَّا مِنْ غِسْلِينٍ . لَا يَأْكُلُهُ إِلَّا الْخَاطِئُونَ}$$

" As for the one who receives his record in the left hand, he will
say, "Oh dear! If only I were not given my record and I had not
known my reckoning! Alas! If only death had been my end. My
wealth has not helped me and my kingship has been destroyed."
(Addressing the angels of punishment, Allāh will say,) "Grab
him and place a yoke around his neck! Then enter him into the
Blaze! Then fasten him in a chain seventy cubits in length. Verily he did not encourage feeding the poor. There shall neither be
any friend for him today (to assist him) nor any food except the
filth (that) remains after washing (the puss and blood oozing
from the wounds of the people of Jahannam)." (It is food that)
only the sinners shall eat (in Jahannam) (69:25-37)

Allāh ﷻ continues, **"Do you know what the Day of Retribution
is? Do you really know what the Day of Retribution is?"** People
should therefore be concerned about their plight on the Day of
Judgement. Allāh ﷻ then briefly describes the Day of Judgement
when He says, **"It shall be a Day when one soul will be unable to
benefit another soul in the least. On that Day, all authority will
be Allāhs."**
Although many people have been vested with some authority in
this world, they will all be helpless on the Day of Judgement. They
will have no authority to do anything except desire to be on the
receiving end, requiring assistance from others. However, none
will be able to assist one another.

Allāh ﷻ proclaims His sovereignty of the Day of Judgement to remind mankind of the consequences of his actions in this world.

In one verse, He says,

لِّمَنِ الْمُلْكُ الْيَوْمَ لِلَّهِ الْوَاحِدِ الْقَهَّارِ

"Whose is the kingdom today? (There will be pin drop silence on the Plain of Resurrection, then He will Himself proclaim,) it is Allāh's, the One, the Dominant (40:16)

Likewise in another verse, He says,

اَلْمُلْكُ يَوْمَئِذٍ الْحَقُّ لِلرَّحْمٰنِ

"The true sovereignty on that Day will be for the Most Gracious." (25:26)

Hence, on that Day it will be utter chaos. The Holy Prophet ﷺ said in a Hadeeth of Muslim,

يَا بَنِيْ هَاشِمٍ أَنْقِذُوا أَنْفُسَكُمْ مِّنَ النَّارِ لَا أَمْلِكُ لَكُمْ مِّنَ اللهِ شَيْئًا

"O' Children of Hāshim! Save yourselves from the fire, for I have no power to help you from (the punishment of) Allāh ﷻ." (Muslim)

Allāh ﷻ instilling the fear of that Day says in a verse of Sūrah Al-Baqarah,

وَاتَّقُوا يَوْمًا لَّا تَجْزِيْ نَفْسٌ عَنْ نَفْسٍ شَيْئًا وَّلَا يُقْبَلُ مِنْهَا شَفَاعَةٌ وَّلَا يُؤْخَذُ مِنْهَا

52

عَدْلٌ وَّلَا هُمْ يُنْصَرُوْنَ

"Fear that Day when one soul will not pay anything towards another, no intercession will be accepted, no ransom will be taken and they will not be helped." (2:48)

Normally, in this world, when a person is faced with any difficulty, he tries to overcome it with his own effort. If it doesn't prove successful, he will use a reference or intercession of a person of higher authority. If that doesn't seem to work, he might even resort to bribe and try to overcome the plight that he has fallen into. Ultimately, if this doesn't resolve the problem, he might exceed all limits and utilise force and try to revolt against his opponents or obstacles.

In this verse, Allāh ﷻ negates all four avenues and proclaims that nothing will avail him from the horrors of that Day. Firstly, he himself will not be able to avail himself from the punishment, secondly, no intercession, thirdly, no ransom and fourthly, no strength or power will be able to overturn the decision made by Allāh ﷻ.

A point to remember here at this juncture is that, this verse does not negate intercession, because that will not happen with one's free will, unless Allāh ﷻ grants permission to someone to intercede on someone's behalf, and then accepts the intercession.

In Āyatul Kursi, He says,

مَنْ ذَا الَّذِيْ يَشْفَعُ عِنْدَه إِلَّا بِإِذْنِه

"Who is there that can intercede before Him without His permission." (2:255)

Sūrah Mutaffifeen

Those Who Cheat
Revealed in Makkah

بِسْمِ اللهِ الرَّحْمٰنِ الرَّحِيْمِ

**In the Name of Allāh, the Most Compassionate, the Most
Merciful**

وَيْلٌ لِّلْمُطَفِّفِيْنَ ۔ الَّذِيْنَ إِذَا اكْتَالُوْا عَلَى النَّاسِ يَسْتَوْفُوْنَ ۔ وَإِذَا كَالُوْهُمْ أَوْ وَزَنُوْهُمْ
يُخْسِرُوْنَ ۔ أَلَا يَظُنُّ أُولَئِكَ أَنَّهُمْ مَّبْعُوْثُوْنَ ۔ لِيَوْمٍ عَظِيْمٍ ۔ يَوْمَ يَقُوْمُ النَّاسُ لِرَبِّ
الْعَالَمِيْنَ

1. Woe to the cheaters.
2. Who when they take measure from mankind, demand in full.
3. But if they measure or weigh for people they reduce.
4. Do such people not consider that they will be raised,
5. For an awful Day,
6. The Day when all of mankind will stand before the Lord of
   the universe?

According to Sayyidunā Abdullāh Ibn Mas'ood ﷺ, Sūrah Mutaffifeen was revealed in Makkah. Therefore, most of the copies of
the Holy Qur'ān refer to it as a Makki Sūrah.

According to Sayyidunā Abdullāh Ibn Abbās ﷺ, it is a Madani
Sūrah but only about eight verses are Makki. Sayyidunā Abdullāh
Ibn Abbās ﷺ narrates that when the Holy Prophet ﷺ migrated to

Madeenah Munawwarah, the inhabitants of Madeenah Munawwarah, whose most transactions were based on measurements, used to cheat and measure short. For this reason, Allāh ﷻ revealed this Sūrah. Furthermore, Sayyidunā Abdullāh Ibn Abbās ؓ states that this is the first Sūrah that was revealed as soon as the Holy Prophet ﷺ migrated to Madeenah Munawwarah.

The reason is that it was such a common practice in Madeenah Munawwarah that the people used to be extremely strict in measuring when they had to receive something from the seller, but in the reverse they used to cheat the buyers. After the revelation of this Sūrah, all of them abandoned this custom totally and mended themselves in a way that they became well known in their honesty of weighing and measuring. (Nasai, Ibn Mājah)

Sūrah Mutaffifeen is also called Sūrah Tatfeef. The word 'Tatfeef' refers to reducing or diminishing quantities when weighing or measuring (i.e. cheating). A common method of measuring quantities of grain in previous times was by filling utensils of standardised sizes.

Woe to the Cheaters

وَيْلٌ لِّلْمُطَفِّفِينَ

Woe to the cheaters

The above verses condemn the act of people cheating when weighing or measuring. Allāh ﷻ speaks of people who cheat others that buy from them and that when they buy from others, they watch carefully to see that they are given their share in full. Allāh ﷻ reminds such people of the Day of Judgement when they will be taken to task for their misdeeds and will be punished accordingly.

The word وَيْلٌ means woe i.e. destruction or punishment to the curtailers and cheaters. Another meaning which has been mentioned in Tafseer Jalālain is that وَيْلٌ is a valley in Jahannam where a disbeliever will be punished. It is so gigantic and huge that if a disbeliever is thrown into the valley of وَيْلٌ, it will take 40 years to reach its bottom.

May Allāh ﷻ save us all. Āmeen!

Allāh ﷻ has commanded us to carry out the measure and weight accurately in all types of transactions.

Allāh ﷻ says,

وَأَوْفُوا الْكَيْلَ إِذَا كِلْتُمْ وَزِنُوا بِالْقِسْطَاسِ الْمُسْتَقِيمِ ذَٰلِكَ خَيْرٌ وَأَحْسَنُ تَأْوِيلًا

"Measure in full when you measure (goods for people) and weigh with proper scales so that others are not cheated. This is the best and better in the final outcome (because it leads to mutual trust and rules out disputes)." (17:35)

In another verse, He says,

وَأَوْفُوا الْكَيْلَ وَالْمِيزَانَ بِالْقِسْطِ لَا نُكَلِّفُ نَفْسًا إِلَّا وُسْعَهَا

"And give full measure and weight in fairness (when you trade
with people). We do not place on a soul a responsibility unless it
is within its capability." (6:152)

In Sūrah Rahmān, Allāh ﷻ says,

وَأَقِيمُوا الْوَزْنَ بِالْقِسْطِ وَلَا تُخْسِرُوا الْمِيزَانَ

"And observe weight with equity and do not make the balance
deficient." (55:09)

The punishment of the sin for cheating in weight and measure is
also experienced in this world. Sayyidunā Abdullāh Ibn Abbās ؓ
reports that the Holy Prophet ﷺ said to those who cheat in weighing and measuring that they are committing a sin that caused people of previous nations to be destroyed in this very world.
(Mishkāt)

Sayyidunā Abdullāh Ibn Abbās ؓ states in Muwatta of Imām
Mālik ؓ that sustenance is constrained for those who cheat in
weight and measure. This means that they will either be given less
sustenance or that they will be deprived of blessings in their sustenance.

It is Harām to give a customer less than the weight or the measurement for which he has paid for. On the contrary, the Shari'ah has
encouraged traders to give the customer more than what he pays
for.

The Holy Prophet ﷺ was once passing a person who was employed to measure for a trader. The Holy Prophet ﷺ said to him, "Measure and give more."

The nation of Sayyidunā Shuaib عليه السلام started the evil practice of cheating in weight and measure. Despite his persistent efforts to reform them, the people refused to desist from this evil. Eventually, Allāh's ﷻ punishment destroyed them.

Sayyidunā Shuaib عليه السلام conveyed the message of Allāh ﷻ to them and cautioned them of cheating in weight and measure.

أَوْفُوا الْكَيْلَ وَلَا تَكُونُوا مِنَ الْمُخْسِرِينَ ۚ وَزِنُوا بِالْقِسْطَاسِ الْمُسْتَقِيمِ ۚ وَلَا تَبْخَسُوا النَّاسَ أَشْيَاءَهُمْ وَلَا تَعْثَوْا فِي الْأَرْضِ مُفْسِدِينَ ۚ وَاتَّقُوا الَّذِي خَلَقَكُمْ وَالْجِبِلَّةَ الْأَوَّلِينَ ۚ قَالُوا إِنَّمَا أَنْتَ مِنَ الْمُسَحَّرِينَ ۚ وَمَا أَنْتَ إِلَّا بَشَرٌ مِثْلُنَا وَإِنْ نَظُنُّكَ لَمِنَ الْكَاذِبِينَ ۚ فَأَسْقِطْ عَلَيْنَا كِسَفًا مِنَ السَّمَاءِ إِنْ كُنْتَ مِنَ الصَّادِقِينَ ۚ قَالَ رَبِّي أَعْلَمُ بِمَا تَعْمَلُونَ ۚ فَكَذَّبُوهُ فَأَخَذَهُمْ عَذَابُ يَوْمِ الظُّلَّةِ إِنَّهُ كَانَ عَذَابَ يَوْمٍ عَظِيمٍ ۚ إِنَّ فِي ذَلِكَ لَآيَةً وَمَا كَانَ أَكْثَرُهُمْ مُؤْمِنِينَ ۚ وَإِنَّ رَبَّكَ لَهُوَ الْعَزِيزُ الرَّحِيمُ

"Measure (the commodities you sell) in full and do not be of those who reduce (the amount of goods being sold while accepting full payments for it) and weigh (what you sell by weight) with a just balance (without cheating your customer) in any way." Do not reduce people's goods (by giving them less than what they paid for) and do not spread corruption on earth (by

robbing people and devouring their rights).

"Fear the Being Who created you and all the previous creations." They said, "You must surely be one of the (heavily) bewitched ones. You are merely a human like ourselves (you are no better than us, so why should we obey you?) In fact, we consider you (certainly to be less than a human like us because you are) from the liars."

"So cause a piece of the sky to fall on us as (a punishment) if you are from the truthful ones? (if you are really a Messenger and if your warnings of punishment are true and not mere threats). He (Shuaib said), "My Lord knows best what you do." (He knows everything you do and therefore knows what punishment you deserve and exactly when the punishment should arrive). So, they (utterly) rejected him and the punishment of the day of the canopy seized them. It was certainly a punishment of a dreadful day. (Allāh made the weather extremely hot, all the people left their homes and sought shelter beneath the trees. Then, Allāh sent a dense cloud towards them, which they mistook for a 'canopy' to escape from the heat. When they gathered beneath the cloud, a descending fire scorched them all). There is certainly a great sign (lesson) in this. However, most of them do not have Imān (even after listening to these truthful events). Verily your Lord is Mighty (Powerful enough to destroy whoever He wills), the Most Merciful (Most Forgiving to whoever repents sincerely). (26:181-191)

Different Forms of Tatfeef (Cheating)

The Holy Qur'ān and Sunnah has prohibited Tatfeef, which primarily signifies giving less in measure and weight because generally all transactions are carried out by things that can be measured and weighed. The basic purpose of weighing or measuring is nothing else but to give a person what he deserves, hence it indicates that the rule is not restricted to weights and measures but it encompasses all other means through which rights of someone are evaluated and assessed. It is obligatory that all rights are given to the deserving person in full, whether they are assessed by weight, measure, number or any other means. In terms of this concept of Tatfeef, it is prohibited to give a person less than his due.

It is narrated by Imām Mālik 🙵 in his Muwatta that Sayyidunā Umar 🙵 saw a person curtailing (cutting short) his Ruku (bowing) and Sajdah (prostration) in Salāh, he reprimanded him by calling out,

$$\text{لَقَدۡ طَفَّفۡتَ}$$

"You have committed Tatfeef (curtailed the right) of Allāh 🙵."

Imām Mālik 🙵 infers the following ruling. "Everything can either be completed properly or one may cheat in completing it."

Cheating can take place in several other ways as well, such as:

- Omitting the Sunnah acts of Salāh
- Omitting the Sunnah acts of Hajj and Umrah.

- Fasting without abstaining from sins like backbiting.
- Reciting the Holy Qur'ān incorrectly.
- Not paying Zakāt in full.

While one will be depriving oneself of the complete rewards for the deeds, certain acts may completely nullify one's good deeds e.g reciting the Holy Qur'ān incorrectly in Salāh may nullify one's Salāh.

Another form of Tatfeef (cheating) is when an employee is employed to work for an agreed number of hours but accepts his full salary for working fewer hours. An employee is obliged to do the work he is being paid for. It is Harām for one to accept one's full salary when the desired work is incomplete or incorrect. An employee will be guilty of 'Tatfeef' if he uses his working hours to engage in activities that are not related to his work like smoking or gossiping. It is unfortunately the practice of many employees to work diligently while the employer is watching but to engage in something else when his back is turned. The person doing this, is guilty of 'Tatfeef'.

Also guilty of 'Tatfeef' is the employee who does something contrary to what he is paid for and who accepts a bribe to do something due to the position of his employment. While the bribe is in itself Harām, part of his salary will become Harām for him because he is not doing what he is being paid for.

Five Punishments for Five Sins

Sayyidunā Abdullāh Ibn Abbās ؓ has narrated that the Holy Prophet ﷺ has said, "There are five sins for which there are five punishments.

1. He who breaks the covenant (pledge) of Allāh ﷻ will cause his enemy to subdue him.
2. The nation that abandons the sacred laws of Allāh ﷻ and decides cases according to other laws, poverty will prevail commonly among them.
3. The nation among whom promiscuity and Zinā (adultery and fornication) becomes rampant, Allāh ﷻ will punish them with epidemic and endemic diseases.
4. Those who curtail measures and weights, Allāh ﷻ will cause famine to break out amongst them.
5. Those who fail to pay their Zakāt, Allāh ﷻ will withhold rain from them.

In another narration, reported by Imām Tabarani ؓ that Sayyidunā Abdullāh Ibn Abbās ؓ reports from the Holy Prophet ﷺ who said,

1. "When stealing from the spoils of war becomes rampant in a community, then Allāh ﷻ will cast the terror of the enemies into their hearts.
2. When worry becomes a common practice in a community, death becomes a frequent occurrence in that society.
3. A community that gives less in measure and weight, Allāh ﷻ cuts off their sustenance.

4.   Those who decide against the truth, murder becomes com-
      mon among them.
5.   Those who betray their agreement, Allāh ﷻ causes their ene-
      mies to prevail over them." (Muwatta Imām Mālik)

Shaykh Abul Qāsim Qushairi ﷜ has mentioned that from the many
forms of Tatfeef, some of them are:

*   Exposing the faults of others whilst having faults in oneself.
*   Demanding justice from others whilst oneself being unjust.
*   Looking at the shortcomings of others and not focusing on
    ones own shortcomings.
*   Desiring respect and honour from others and not giving due
    respect to those who are highly respectable.
*   Not to desire for others what one desires for oneself.
*   To demand full and complete work from the employees but
    to be late in paying their wages.
*   To ask for Rizq (sustenance) from Allāh ﷻ but to fall short in
    His obedience.

Regarding transactions of this nature where measurement and
weight is concerned, there are four types of people:

1.   He fulfils the weight whilst giving and taking.
2.   He reduces and curtails in both giving and taking.
3.   He reduces whilst giving but demands in full when receiving.
      This is the type mentioned in the Holy Qur'ān.
4.   He gives in full and takes less. This is the best type.

The first two types are not mentioned because even though they are wrong and prohibited they are not evil to the highest degree. In the first instance, the extra taking will be in exchange of extra giving and in the second instance, the reduction and shortage in taking will be in exchange of the shortage in giving.

Horrors of Judgement Day

"Do such people not consider that they will be raised unto an awful Day, the Day when all mankind will stand before the Lord of the universe?"

Allāh ﷻ threatens the Mutaffifeen (the cheaters) with standing before the Lord of the universe, Who knows the hidden matters and the innermost secrets on a Day that contains great horrors and tremendous fright. Whoever loses on this Day will be made to enter a blazing fire. Mankind will stand barefooted, naked and uncircumcised at a station that will be difficult, hard and distressful for the criminals.

Imām Bukhāri ﷺ and Imām Muslim ﷺ both narrate a Hadeeth in their respective books from Sayyidunā Abdullāh Ibn Umar ؓ that the Holy Prophet ﷺ said, "This will be the Day that mankind will stand before the Lord of all that exists, until one of them will sink up to the middle of his ears in sweat."

In another Hadeeth narrated by Imām Muslim ؓ and Imām Tirmizi ؓ, it mentions that the Holy Prophet ﷺ said,

65

"On the Day of Judgement, the sun will draw near the servants until it is a mile or two away from them. Then the sun will burn them and they will be submersed in sweat based upon the amount of their deeds. From amongst them, there will be those whose sweat will come up to their knees. From among them, there will be those whose sweat will come up to their groins. From among them, there will be those who will be bridled in sweat up to their necks." (Muslim, Tirmizi)

In Sunan Abū Dāwood, it is recorded that the Holy Prophet ﷺ used to seek refuge in Allāh ﷻ, from the hardship of standing on the Day of Judgement. It has been reported from Sayyidunā Abdullāh Ibn Mas'ood ؓ that the people will be standing for forty years with their heads raised towards the sky. No one will speak to them and the righteous and wicked among them will all be bridled in sweat.

Sayyidah Āishah ؓ narrates that the Holy Prophet ﷺ used to begin his late night prayer (Tahajjud) by declaring Allāh's ﷻ greatness ten times and seeking Allāh's ﷻ forgiveness ten times. He then would say,

$$ اَللّٰهُمَّ اغْفِرْ لِيْ وَاهْدِنِيْ وَارْزُقْنِيْ وَعَافِنِيْ $$

"O' Allāh! Forgive me, guide me, provide for me and protect me."

Then he would seek refuge from the hardship of standing on the Day of Judgment.

Every individual should be concerned about this horrific Day when he will have to account for all his deeds before Allāh ﷻ and will have to suffer the punishment for his sins. By constantly keeping this in mind, Inshā'Allāh one will neither violate the rights one owes to Allāh ﷺ nor those that he owes to fellow men. The factor that contributes most towards sins is man's negligence towards the Day of Judgment.

Coming back to the verse, **"Do such people not consider that (after death) they will be raised unto an awful (mighty) Day (Qiyāmah)."**

In this verse, Allāh ﷺ uses a question of reproach, admonishing the people who perpetrate these sins of not considering the accounts they have to give Allāh ﷺ on that petrifying day.

Furthermore, Allāh ﷺ used the word ظَنَّ 'consider and think' implying that every intelligent person has full certitude of this Day but those wretched people don't have the slightest consideration or thought. Having any certitude and conviction is far-fetched for these people.

Secondly, the word ظَنَّ implies that even if an individual doesn't have the conviction but has some consideration of Judgement Day then that would have sufficed him to refrain from these detestable acts. A traveller just on the speculation that there will be no food or drink available during the journey will carry his provisions with him in case of an emergency, but this foolish person will not even consider that he will need to stand in front of Allāh ﷺ on that mighty and awful Day.

Sayyidunā Abdullāh Ibn Umar ﷺ, one day commenced with the recitation of Sūrah Mutaffifeen in his Salāh. When he recited the verse,

$$\text{يَوْمَ يَقُوْمُ النَّاسُ لِرَبِّ الْعَالَمِيْنَ}$$

"The Day when all mankind will stand before the Lord of the universe (to account for their actions and words)."

he became unconscious and fell down due to extreme fear. Allāhu-Akbar!

$$\text{كَلَّا إِنَّ كِتَابَ الْفُجَّارِ لَفِيْ سِجِّيْنٍ . وَمَا أَدْرَاكَ مَا سِجِّيْنٌ . كِتَابٌ مَّرْقُوْمٌ . وَيْلٌ يَّوْمَئِذٍ لِّلْمُكَذِّبِيْنَ . الَّذِيْنَ يُكَذِّبُوْنَ بِيَوْمِ الدِّيْنِ . وَمَا يُكَذِّبُ بِهِ إِلَّا كُلُّ مُعْتَدٍ أَثِيْمٍ . إِذَا تُتْلَى عَلَيْهِ آيَاتُنَا قَالَ أَسَاطِيْرُ الْأَوَّلِيْنَ . كَلَّا بَلْ رَانَ عَلَى قُلُوْبِهِمْ مَّا كَانُوْا يَكْسِبُوْنَ . كَلَّا إِنَّهُمْ عَنْ رَّبِّهِمْ يَوْمَئِذٍ لَّمَحْجُوْبُوْنَ . ثُمَّ إِنَّهُمْ لَصَالُو الْجَحِيْمِ . ثُمَّ يُقَالُ هٰذَا الَّذِيْ كُنْتُمْ بِهِ تُكَذِّبُوْنَ}$$

8. It shall never be! Verily the records of the sinners shall be in 'Sijjeen'

9. How will you know what the record places in 'Sijjeen' are?

10. A sealed book.

11. May misery be the lot of the deniers on that Day.

12. Those who deny the Day of Retribution

13. It is only every sinful transgressor who denies it.

14. When our verses are recited to him, he says, "These are fables of the men of old."

68

15. Never! In fact, the rust of their sins has covered their hearts.
16. Never! They will certainly be veiled from (seeing) their Lord on that Day.
17. They will definitely enter Jahannam.
18. Thereafter it will be said, "This is what you used to deny!"

Sijjeen

Allāh ﷻ confirms, **"It shall never be!"** i.e it shall never be as the disbelievers think that the Day of Judgement will not take place. The Day of Judgement will certainly take place. Men should never think that his words and deeds have disappeared into thin air and that he is not required to account for them. Indeed the records of every person's deeds are preserved.

The word 'Sijjeen' is derived from 'Sajana,' which means to imprison in a narrow place. According to Qāmus, the word Sijjeen means eternal imprisonment.

From the Ahādeeth, it indicates that Sijjeen is a specific place where the souls of the disbelievers are kept and in the same place, the records of the evil deeds of every wicked person are kept separately.

Where is this place? According to a lengthy Hadeeth reported by Sayyidunā Barā Ibn Āzib ؓ that the Holy Prophet ﷺ said, "Allāh ﷻ says concerning the soul of the disbeliever, "Record his book in Sijjeen." And Sijjeen is beneath the seventh earth. (Tabarāni, Hākim)

It is known that the destination of the evil people will be Hell and it is the lowest of the low, for Allāh ﷻ says,

ثُمَّ رَدَدْنَاهُ أَسْفَلَ سَافِلِيْنَ . إِلَّا الَّذِيْنَ آمَنُوْا وَعَمِلُوا الصَّالِحَاتِ

"Then We returned him to the lowest of the low, save those who believe and do righteous deeds." (95:5-6)

The Location of Paradise and Hell

Imām Baihaqi ﷺ has recorded a narration from Sayyidunā Abdullāh Ibn Salām ؓ that Paradise is in the Heaven and Hell is in the earth. Ibn Jareer ﷺ cites in his commentary on the authority of Sayyidunā Mu'ādh Ibn Jabal ؓ, a narration of the Holy Prophet ﷺ according to which he was asked about the meaning of the following verse,

وَجِيْءَ يَوْمَئِذٍ بِجَهَنَّمَ

"And Jahannam (Hell) on that Day will be brought forward." (89:23)

The Holy Prophet ﷺ was asked, "Where will Hell be brought forward from? He replied, "From the seventh earth." These narrations indicate that Hell will be brought forward from the seventh earth. It will suddenly flare up and all the oceans will join its blazing fire and come forward in full view of everyone.

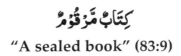

كِتَابٌ مَّرْقُوْمٌ

"A sealed book" (83:9)

The word 'Marqoom' literally means 'inscribed' but translated here as 'sealed'.

Ibn Katheer ﷺ says that this statement is not the interpretation of Sijjeen but rather the explanation of a phrase before that,

$$إِنَّ كِتَابَ الْفُجَّارِ لَفِي سِجِّينٍ$$

"Indeed the record of deeds of the sinners is in Sijjeen." (83:7)

It is both inscribed and sealed. No one can add anything to it, nor can anyone remove anything from it and nor is any alteration possible on it. The place where it is kept for safe custody is called Sijjeeen and it is placed where the souls of the disbelievers are gathered.

Allāh ﷺ continues, **"May misery be the lot of the deniers on that Day, those who deny the Day of Retribution. It is only every sinful transgressor who denies it. When Our verses are recited to him, he says," These are fables of the men of old." Never! (The Qur'ān can never be a fable) In fact, the rust of their sins has covered their hearts."**

<u>Rust on the Hearts</u>

The disbelievers evil deeds, especially their Kufr (disbelief) and Shirk (polytheism) have covered their hearts with rust that prevents the truth from penetrating. Therefore they cannot understand the truth and persist in rebellion.

The word رَانَ 'Rāna' is derived from رَيْنَ 'Raina' and it means rust, dust or filth. In other words, the rust of committing many sins have covered up their hearts just as rust consumes the iron and turns into dust. Similarly, the rust of their sins has destroyed their innate capacity to distinguish right from wrong.

In Arabic terminology, 'Rāna' is used for the dark covering which overcomes the hearts of the disbelievers. The word غَيْمٌ 'Ghaym' is the covering which overcomes the hearts of the believers. There is another word غَيْنٌ 'Ghayn', which comes for the covering of those who are near and closest to Allāh ﷻ. Hence in a Hadeeth narrated by Imām Muslim ﷺ says that the Holy Prophet ﷺ said,

"Indeed a form of contamination settles to my heart and I repent to Allāh ﷻ a hundred times daily." (Muslim)

This happened due to the Holy Prophet's ﷺ status and rank increasing every moment and when he reflected on his previous rank, he recited Istighfār for any shortcomings. Only Allāh ﷻ knows best!

Sayyidunā Abū Hurairah ﷺ narrates that the Holy Prophet ﷺ said,

"Verily when a servant commits a sin, a black spot appears in his heart. If he repents from it, his heart is polished clean. However, if he increases (in the sin) the spot will continue to increase. This is the statement of Allāh ﷻ: **Nay! But in their hearts is the rust (covering) which they used to earn.**" (Tirmizi)

72

In a Hadeeth of Nasai, it says,

"Whenever the servant commits a wrong, a black spot is put in his heart. So, if he refrains from it, seeks forgiveness from it and repents, his heart is polished clean. But if he returns to the sin, the spot will increase until it overcomes his (entire) heart and this is the rust (covering) that Allāh ﷻ mentions when He says, **"Nay! But on their hearts is the rust (covering) which they used to earn."**

The particle, ﻛَﻼّ in Arabic grammar is called 'Harf-ur-rad', particle of disapproval, particle of repelling or averting. In the preceding verses, it mentioned the attitude of the disbelievers towards the Qur'anic verses that when they are revealed to them, they say, "These are tales of the men of old." The present verse uses ﻛَﻼّ 'Never' to repel the false idea of the ignorant ones who claim that the Holy Qur'ān is the tale of the old. In fact, the heavy burden of their sins have eclipsed the light and innate capacity to separate the right and the wrong. This capacity is innate and inborn in man. The verse intends to say that their rejection is not based on any logical or intellectual evidence but their hearts have become blind and as a result they are unable to distinguish between the good and the bad.

The Holy Prophet ﷺ has prescribed Tawbah (repentance) as the cure for the rust that settles on the heart. One should therefore resort to Tawbah as soon as one commits a sin so that the heart is never covered by rust which prevents one from distinguishing falsehood from the truth.

Allāh's ﷻ Vision

Concerning the plight of those who deny the Day of Judgement, Allāh ﷻ says, **"Never! They will certainly be veiled from seeing their Lord on that Day. They will definitely enter Jahannam." Thereafter it will be said, "This is what you used to deny."**

This will be their punishment in the future i.e. the Hereafter, for not recognising Allāh ﷻ in this world. The disbelievers will remain deprived of seeing Allāh ﷻ that on the Day of Judgement a screen will fall between them and Allāh ﷻ. Imām Shāfi'ee and Imām Mālik ﷺ state that in this verse, there is proof that the true believers will be able to see Allāh ﷻ, otherwise the statement that the disbelievers will be screened off from their Lord on the Day of Judgement will have no real meaning.

According to some learned predecessors, this verse is a proof that man by virtue of his innate nature has love for Allāh ﷻ, His Creator, hence all the disbelievers in the world no matter how deeply they are stooped in their form of disbelief or hold false beliefs regarding the Supreme Being and attributes of Allāh ﷻ, there is a common denominator in their hearts that they love and respect their Creator, Allāh ﷻ. It is a separate matter that they have taken the wrong path which will ultimately take them to the Hellfire.

The reason our pious predecessors put forward is that if they did not have the desire to see their Lord, it would not have been said in their punishment that they will remain deprived of seeing Allāh ﷻ, because if a person is not desirous of seeing Him, it would be no punishment for him.

A disbeliever may speculate that on the Day of Judgement the rust which covered their hearts will be cleaned and polished by the Divine light and by the sight of Allāh 🕮, but Allāh 🕮 refutes their speculation in this verse by saying, "Never!" It will never occur, hence, that rust which was not removed in the Dunya (world) it will become permanent on the Day of Judgement.

According to the Ahlus-Sunnah Wal Jamā'at, the people of Jannah will be able to see Allāh 🕮. In fact, the greatest blessing in Jannah will be the actual vision of Allāh 🕮 by the people of Jannah. Allāh 🕮 states,

$$ وُجُوْهٌ يَّوْمَئِذٍ نَّاضِرَةٌ ۚ إِلَى رَبِّهَا نَاظِرَةٌ $$

"The Day when faces will be radiant looking at their Lord." (75:22-23)

This verse clearly refers to the vision of Allāh 🕮." It is narrated by Sayyidunā Suhaib Rūmi 🕮 that the Holy Prophet 🕮 said, "When the righteous people will enter Jannah, Allāh 🕮 will enquire from them, "Do you desire that we grant you one more favour?" (i.e. bestow upon you a blessing in addition to what you already have received).

They will reply, "How? You have illuminated our faces and saved us from Jahannam and granted us Jannah. What more can we ask for?"

The veil will then be lifted and they will be able to see Allāh 🕮.

This blessing will surpass all other blessings that have been bestowed upon them.

Thereafter, the Holy Prophet ﷺ recited the following verse from the Holy Qur'ān,

"For those who do good deeds shall be the best place and even more." (10:26)

In this verse, al-Husnā (best place) refers to Jannah and Ziyādah (even more) refers to having the honour of seeing Allāh ﷻ Himself.

It is reported in Bukhāri and Muslim that the Holy Prophet ﷺ has said, "You will see your Lord clearly."

Sayyidunā Jābir Ibn Abdullāh ؓ narrates, "One night we were sitting with the Holy Prophet ﷺ when he looked up at the moon. It was shining in the sky. The Holy Prophet ﷺ then turned towards us and said, "Surely, you will see Allāh ﷻ as you are seeing the moon. You will not need to make special efforts to see Him nor will there be any other difficulty." (Bukhāri, Muslim)

This great blessing of the vision of Allāh ﷻ will be granted to the believers according to their ranks. The general believers will be able to see Allāh ﷻ on a weekly basis on a Friday which will be called Yawmul-Mazeed. Those who are close to Allāh ﷻ will be able to see Him twice daily - once after Fajr Salāh and once after Asr Salāh. Those who are the most closest will have the privilege and opportunity to see Him all the time. May Allāh ﷻ bless us with His vision and count us from the closest ones, Āmeen!

Sayyidunā Mūsā ﷺ requested Allāh ﷻ,

"O my Lord, show me (Yourself so) that I may see You," Allāh replied, "You can never see Me (in this world) but look at the mountain. If it remains in place (after a tiny fraction of My illumination reaching it) then you may (have the ability to) see Me. (However) when his Lord manifested His illumination to the mountain, He made it crush to pieces and (seeing the marvellous spectacle) Sayyidunā Mūsā fell unconscious. (7:143)

This verse indicates that it is not possible to see Allāh ﷻ because a human body will not be able to endure the mighty illumination of Allāh ﷻ; but if we ponder over this verse, we will come to the conclusion that the شَرْط (Shart - Condition) - "If it remains in its place then you may see Me," has been put forward here which is not possible in this world.

In a verse of Sūrah Furqān, Allāh ﷻ mentions the Jazā (the result) which will be in the Hereafter.

$$ أَصْحَابُ الْجَنَّةِ يَوْمَئِذٍ خَيْرٌ مُّسْتَقَرًّا وَأَحْسَنُ مَقِيلًا $$

"The People of Jannah will be in the best of abodes and the best of resting places." (25:24)

Hence this abode of steadfastness and permanent residence will be found in Paradise which will result in the vision of Allāh ﷻ. The famous Arabic grammar ruling is, 'When the Shart (condition) is found, then the Jazā (result) (i.e. the vision of Allāh ﷻ) will also be found.'

Those who will be deprived of seeing Allāh ﷻ will be regretting over their deprivation and loss. That is not the end of it - those who might think that what is the big deal if we cannot see our Lord, for them Allāh ﷻ says, **"Then (in addition to this) they will definitely enter (fall into) Jahannam. Thereafter, (once they have entered Jahannam) it will be said, "This (punishment of Jahannam) is what you used to deny (in this world)."**

$$ كَلَّا إِنَّ كِتَابَ الْأَبْرَارِ لَفِي عِلِّيِّينَ . وَمَا أَدْرَاكَ مَا عِلِّيُّونَ . كِتَابٌ مَّرْقُومٌ . يَشْهَدُهُ الْمُقَرَّبُونَ $$

18. It shall never be! Verily the records of the righteous shall be in Illiyyūn.
19. How will you know what the records placed in Illiyyūn are?
20. A sealed book,
21. which the close angels witness.

Allāh ﷻ states, **"It shall be never be!"** i.e. it shall never be as the disbelievers think that the Day of Judgement will not take place because it certainly will. People should refrain from thinking that their words and actions have disappeared into thin air and that they are not required to account for them. Indeed, every person's deeds are recorded.

Illiyyūn

Allāh ﷻ says, "**Verily the record of every righteous will be in Illiyyūn. How will you know what the records placed in Illiyyūn are? It is a sealed book which the close angels witness.**"

According to some commentators, Illiyyūn is the plural of 'Uluww' and it signifies the highest point. According to the great grammarian Imām Farrā ﷺ, this is the name of a place - it is however, not plural but on the measure of plural. When analysing the word Sijjeen in the foregoing paragraphs, the Hadeeth of Sayyidunā Barā Ibn Āzib ؓ explains that "Illiyyūn is a place on the seventh heaven beneath the Divine Throne where the souls of the believers and the registers of deeds are kept. The phrase كِتَابٌ مَّرْقُومٌ (a sealed book) is not the interpretation of Illiyyūn, but rather the explanation of the phrase before that, i.e. the destination that will be recorded for them is Illiyyūn.

Ibn Katheer ﷺ writes Illiyyūn is located at Sidratul Muntahā. This is the last tree of the upmost boundary of the seventh heaven beyond which none can pass. The obvious meaning of the word Illiyyūn is taken from the word 'Uluww' which mean highness. The more something ascends and rises, the more it becomes greater and increases. Thus Allāh ﷻ magnifies it and exalts its status by saying,

$$\text{وَمَا أَدْرَاكَ مَا عِلِّيُّونَ}$$

"**How will you know what the records placed in Illiyyūn are?**"

79

يَشْهَدُهُ الْمُقَرَّبُوْنَ

"Which the close angels witness".

The verb 'Yash hadu' is derived from 'Shuhood' which means to attend, to witness, to be present, to observe. The verse is explaining that the record of deeds of the righteous will be in the custody of Angels who are blessed with nearness to Allāh ﷻ (Qurtubi)

If 'Shuhood' is taken in the sense of being present then the attached pronoun will refer to 'Illiyyūn' instead of 'Kutub' or register (and those who are blessed with nearness to Allāh ﷻ will refer to the righteous people, and not the angels), and the verse in that case will mean: the souls of those blessed with nearness to Allāh ﷻ will be in the place called Illiyyūn, because that is the abode of the pious souls, and Sijjeen is the abode of the disbelievers.

Sayyidunā Abdullāh Ibn Mas'ood ؓ narrates a Hadeeth in which the Holy Prophet ﷺ said,

"The souls of the martyrs are in crops (groups) of green birds, enjoying the rivers and goodness of Paradise, and their abode will be the lamps suspended from the Divine Throne." (Muslim).

This indicates that the soul of the martyrs will be under the Divine Throne and will be able to stroll in Paradise.

In another Hadeeth narrated by Sayyidunā K'ab Ibn Mālik ؓ states that the Holy Prophet ﷺ said, "The soul of the believer is a bird that will be hanging in the tree of Paradise until it returns to its body on the Day of Judgement."

The Abode of Human Souls after Death

Regarding the abode of human souls, there are different types of reports. Some suggest that the souls of the disbelievers are in Sijjeen which is below the seventh earth, and the souls of the believers are in Illiyyūn which is in the seventh heaven beneath the Divine Throne. Some Ahādeeth indicates that the souls of the believers will be in Paradise and the souls of the disbelievers will be in Hell. Some Ahādeeth furthermore suggests that the souls will be in the graves.

Describing the death of the believers and the disbelievers, the Holy Prophet ﷺ said,

"When the Angel of Death removes the soul of a believer, he addresses it saying, "O pure soul, emerge towards Allāh's ﷻ forgiveness and pleasure."

Consequently, the soul emerges as easily as water emerges from a water bag without wasting a moment, the other angels take the soul from the hands of the Angel of Death and place it in the shroud of Jannah and perfume it with the fragrances of Jannah. The Holy Prophet ﷺ mentioned that this fragrance is better than the best fragrances of this world. They then ascend with it to the heavens. Each time they pass by a gathering of angels, they are asked, "Who is this pure soul?" Taking the best names used in the world, they furnish the name of the person with his father's name.

The Holy Prophet ﷺ continued to say that they then approach the doors of the first heaven, which is opened upon their request. In this manner, they reach the seventh heaven with the soul. Upon reaching there, Allāh ﷻ tells them,

"Place the record of my slave in Illiyyūn and return to the earth, because I have created him from the earth, shall return him to it and will resurrect him from it."

He is returned to the grave where he will reply to all the questions. Then the Holy Prophet ﷺ mentions all the bounties that the believer will receive in the grave. Thereafter, the Holy Prophet ﷺ mentioned the death of a disbeliever. He said that when a disbeliever leaves this world for the Hereafter, dark faced angels descend from the heavens, carrying with them a piece of cloth appearing before him as far as the eye can see. Then the Angel of Death comes himself, sits by the head and says, "O' foul soul, emerge towards Allāh's ﷻ anger!" The soul then disperses throughout the body in an attempt to escape. Thereafter the Angel of Death forcefully extracts the soul just as wet wool wrapped around a skewer is forcefully removed.

When the Angel of Death removes the soul, the other angels without losing a split second, grab hold of the soul and wrap it in the cloth. Such a foul odour emanates from the soul that does not emanate from any decomposed body on earth. They then take this soul upon the heavens and whenever they pass any group of angels they ask, "Who is this foul soul?" using the worst names on earth. They reply, "This is so and so, son of so and so, (taking the person's name)."

When they reach the doors of heavens, they request to enter but the doors do not open. Then the Holy Prophet ﷺ recited the following verse from Sūrah A'rāf,

وَلَا يَدْخُلُونَ الْجَنَّةَ حَتَّى يَلِجَ الْجَمَلُ فِي سَمِّ الْخِيَاطِ

"The doors of Heavens are not opened for them and they will not enter Jannah until a camel passes through the eye of a needle." (7:40)

Thereafter, Allāh ﷻ tells the angels to record the person's name in Sijjeen which lies beneath the lowest earth. The soul is then cast there (Mishkāt).

Imām Ibn Abdul-Barr ﷫ prefers this narrative and believes that the souls of all believers and non-believers remain in their graves. As for the first two types of Ahādeeth, there is no contradiction because after carefully analysing, we understand that Illiyyūn is in the seventh heaven beneath the Divine Throne, and this is exactly the location of Paradise which is clear from the Qur'anic text.

عِنْدَ سِدْرَةِ الْمُنْتَهَى . عِنْدَهَا جَنَّةُ الْمَأْوَى

"At the Sidratul Muntaha (near the lote tree from where the Holy Prophet went on the miraculous journey of Mi'rāj to the furthest Jannah). Close to which is Jannatul Ma'wā (a comfortable dwelling above which is Allāh's Throne)." (53:14-15)

This clearly states that Paradise is near the lote-tree in the upper realm and the Ahādeeth confirm that the lote-tree is in the seventh heaven. This suggests that since the abode of the souls is Illiyyūn, Paradise must be near it. These souls will stroll in and along the gardens of Paradise. Therefore, their abode may be said to be Paradise.

Similarly, the souls of disbelievers remain in Sijjeen which is situated below the seventh earth, and the dwellers of Sijjeen will receive the heat and torture of Hell. Therefore, it would be correct to say that their abode is Hell.

However, the Ahādeeth that informs us that the souls of disbelievers and believers will remain in the grave, is apparently contradictory to the preceding two types of Ahādeeth.
Qādhi Thanā-Ullāh ﷺ in his Tafseer Mazhari has reconciled them. He states, "It is not far fetched to assume that Illiyyūn and Sijjeen are the real abodes of the souls, but they have a special connection with their graves. None besides Allāh ﷻ knows the actual nature of the connection. However, there is the sun and the moon in the sky but their rays fall on the earth and provides it with the light and heat. Similarly, the souls in Illiyyūn and Sijjeen may have some spiritual connection with the graves.

Qādhi Thanā-Ullāh ﷺ explains further, which in a nutshell is: There are two types of souls. The first one is a subtle substance that permeates the human body. Despite being a material substance, it is too subtle to be visible and its other name is Nafs. The second soul is an abstract and non-material and pure essence. The pure

abstract and non-material soul is the life of the first soul and therefore is called the soul of the soul. Both categories are connected to
the human body, but the first type of soul resides in the human
body. When the soul leaves the body, death occurs. The second
type of soul is connected to the body more closely than the first
type, but Allāh ﷻ knows the nature of the connection. The first
soul after death is taken to the heaven and then returned to the
grave. The grave is its abode where it is rewarded and punished.
The abstract soul remains in the Illiyyūn if it is pious or Sijjeen if it
is evil. Nevertheless, the final destination is either Paradise or
Illiyyūn or its opposite Hell or Sijjeen. The abode of the abstract
soul is Illiyyūn or Sijjeen. The souls of the first type, the Nafs, remains in the grave after death; and Allāh ﷻ knows best!

إِنَّ الْأَبْرَارَ لَفِي نَعِيمٍ . عَلَى الْأَرَائِكِ يَنْظُرُونَ . تَعْرِفُ فِي وُجُوهِهِمْ نَضْرَةَ النَّعِيمِ .
يُسْقَوْنَ مِنْ رَحِيقٍ مَّخْتُومٍ . خِتَامُهُ مِسْكٌ وَفِي ذَلِكَ فَلْيَتَنَافَسِ الْمُتَنَافِسُونَ .
وَمِزَاجُهُ مِنْ تَسْنِيمٍ . عَيْنًا يَشْرَبُ بِهَا الْمُقَرَّبُونَ

22. **Verily the righteous shall be enjoying bounties.**
23. **While looking on from couches.**
24. **You will recognise the resplendence of bounties on their**
    faces.
25. **They will be given pure sealed wine to drink.**
26. **The seal of which is musk. It is for this the competitors**
    should compete.
27. **Its mixture shall be of Tasneem.**
28. **A spring from which those close to Allāh shall drink.**

Bounties of Jannah

Allāh ﷻ describes the bounties that the pious bondsmen will enjoy in Jannah. These are people whose records shall be placed in Illiyyūn.

Allāh ﷻ says,

"Verily the righteous shall be enjoying bounties while looking on from couches." (Further), you will recognise the happiness of bounties on their faces."

By merely looking at them, one will realise that they are extremely happy and joyful. Referring to the same joy, Allāh ﷻ says in Sūrah Dahr,

$$\text{فَوَقَاهُمُ اللّٰهُ شَرَّ ذٰلِكَ الْيَوْمِ وَلَقَّاهُمْ نَضْرَةً وَسُرُورًا}$$

"So Allāh shall save them from the evil of that Day and will give them radiance and joy." (76:11).

The joy and happiness that the people of Jannah will enjoy shall be heartfelt and not merely superficial.

Referring to the drinks that they will enjoy, Allāh ﷻ says, **"They will be given pure sealed wine to drink, the seal of which is musk."**
One cannot imagine the exquisite and delicious taste of a wine that has a seal of pure musk. This wine will be such that it will neither intoxicate nor produce any headaches like the wine of this world.

86

Allāh ﷻ says in Sūrah Wāqi'ah,

يَطُوفُ عَلَيْهِمْ وِلْدَانٌ مُّخَلَّدُونَ . بِأَكْوَابٍ وَأَبَارِيقَ وَكَأْسٍ مِّن مَّعِينٍ . لَّا يُصَدَّعُونَ
عَنْهَا وَلَا يُنزِفُونَ

"Youngsters of eternal youth shall wait on them with goblets and jugs filled with flowing wine. Neither will they have headaches with it nor will they be intoxicated." (56:17-19)

Encouraging the believers to do good, Allāh ﷻ says,

"It is for this the competitors should compete." Just as people compete with each other to acquire the commodities of this world, they should do the same to attain the bounties of the Hereafter.

People are foolish to vie with each other for things like wine which intoxicates and produces headaches and bad breath. In addition to this, consuming it makes one sinful and deprives one of the wine of the Hereafter. Like this, all other commodities are also not worth competing for.

The Holy Prophet ﷺ mentioned that the following three people will be unable to enter Jannah:

> 1 - The habitual drunkard.
> 2 - The one who severs ties of kinship.
> 3 - The one who practices witchcraft.

In Ma'āriful Qur'ān, Mufti Shafee Sāhib ﷺ writes, "The word 'Tanāfus' means for a few people to try or gain some 'Nafees' (desirable) things before others can get them. Having mentioned the bounties of Paradise, the attention of the heedless people are drawn to the fact that they are thinking that certain material things are desirable, and therefore they are competing one another to obtain them before others. They are told that the material blessings (after which they are running) are perishable. They should not be made the ultimate goal of life nor the object of competition. Man should be content with what he has for the comfort of the fleeting period of this life. If he loses the materialistic things it should not affect him because it is not a loss that cannot be recovered. However, people with aspirations should aspire, race and compete for the blessings of Paradise, that are perfect and eternal in every possible dimension. How aptly the late poet Akbar has put this point forward.

"Gain and loss - what fraction is this?
What is lost is lost.
What is gained is gained.
Say to the heart, the life is short.
If you wish to remind me, remind me of God (Allāh ﷻ)."

Further describing the drinks of Jannah, Allāh ﷻ says,
"It's mixture shall be of Tasneem. A spring from which those close to Allāh shall drink."

Tasneem is the most excellent and exalted drink for the people of

Paradise. Sayyidunā Abdullāh Ibn Mas'ood ﷺ and Sayyidunā Abdullāh Ibn Abbās ﷺ state that those who are really close to Allāh ﷺ shall have the pure water of Tasneem spring to drink, whereas other inhabitants of Jannah will have only a bit of it mixed with other drinks.

إِنَّ الَّذِيْنَ أَجْرَمُوْا كَانُوْا مِنَ الَّذِيْنَ آمَنُوْا يَضْحَكُوْنَ ۞ وَإِذَا مَرُّوْا بِهِمْ يَتَغَامَزُوْنَ ۞ وَإِذَا انْقَلَبُوْا إِلٰى أَهْلِهِمُ انْقَلَبُوْا فَكِهِيْنَ ۞ وَإِذَا رَأَوْهُمْ قَالُوْا إِنَّ هٰؤُلَاءِ لَضَالُّوْنَ ۞ وَمَا أُرْسِلُوْا عَلَيْهِمْ حَافِظِيْنَ ۞ فَالْيَوْمَ الَّذِيْنَ آمَنُوْا مِنَ الْكُفَّارِ يَضْحَكُوْنَ ۞ عَلَى الْأَرَائِكِ يَنْظُرُوْنَ ۞ هَلْ ثُوِّبَ الْكُفَّارُ مَا كَانُوْا يَفْعَلُوْنَ ۞

29. "Verily those who sin used to laugh at the believers.
30. When they passed by them they used to wink at each other.
31. When they return to their families they return jesting.
32. When they saw them, they used to say, "These people are certainly astray."
33. Yet they were never sent as warders over them.
34. However, today the believers shall laugh at the disbelievers
35. while looking on from couches.
36. The fact is that the disbelievers are punished only for what they did."

Behaviour of the Disbelievers

After describing the bounties of the pious believers, Allāh ﷻ speaks about the way in which the disbelievers behave towards the believers. When they used to see a gathering of poor believers like Sayyidunā Khabbāb ◈, Sayyidunā Bilāl ◈ and others, they used to laugh at them and wink to others indicating that these people claim to be worthy of Paradise, whereas they do not even have clothing to cover themselves properly nor shoes to wear. They would then proceed laughing and jesting in this manner to their families. Concerning the believers, they will also say, "These people are certainly astray." If we review the situation today, it is no better. People who have dislike and hatred for Deen are careless and look with contempt towards the scholars and students of Deen. They behave rudely and sarcastically towards the righteous people exactly in the same manner as the disbelievers used to treat the Companions ◈ in the days of the Holy Prophet ﷺ. There is much solace in the concluding verses for the righteous believers. In a nutshell, never bother about the laughter and mockery of those who are far from the Deen. How well a poet put it:

"So long as we fear people's laughter at us, the people will continue to laugh at us."

In Tafseer Azeezi, Shāh Abdul Azeez ◈ explains the systematic order of the injustice perpetrated by the disbelievers upon the believers. Firstly, the disbelievers laugh at the believers, then they wink and jest at them mockingly followed by speaking ill of them in their absence. Finally, they openly claim that they are misguided.

The reason behind the order and sequence of this situation is that when a person dislikes another person's habit or action he will initially laugh at him. When the hatred increases he will start to introduce him mockingly within his circle of friends so that they can participate with him in mocking and ridiculing him. When the enmity and hatred intensifies, then he starts to mention about him sarcastically and maliciously to his friends and families. Finally and ultimately when the mock and hatred reaches its pinnacle and climax, he openly proclaims in public that these people are completely mad and foolish and that they have become astray. This sequence has been considered in the above mentioned verses.

Allāh ﷻ says that the disbelievers surprisingly behave in this manner whereas, **"They were never sent as warders over them (i.e. over the believers)."** This means that the disbelievers will not be asked whether believers were rightly guided or astray in the Hereafter. Therefore, instead of concerning themselves with the affairs of the believers, the disbelievers ought to worry about their own plight in the Hereafter. Allāh ﷻ says in Sūrah Muminūn,

قَالَ اخْسَـُٔوا فِيهَا وَلَا تُكَلِّمُونِ . إِنَّهُ كَانَ فَرِيقٌ مِنْ عِبَادِي يَقُولُونَ رَبَّنَا آمَنَّا فَاغْفِرْ لَنَا وَارْحَمْنَا وَأَنْتَ خَيْرُ الرَّاحِمِينَ . فَاتَّخَذْتُمُوهُمْ سِخْرِيًّا حَتَّى أَنْسَوْكُمْ ذِكْرِيْ وَكُنْتُمْ مِنْهُمْ تَضْحَكُونَ . إِنِّي جَزَيْتُهُمُ الْيَوْمَ بِمَا صَبَرُوا أَنَّهُمْ هُمُ الْفَائِزُونَ

"Remain disgraced (cursed) in it (in Jahannam) and do not speak to me (about being delivered from it)! Do you not remember that there was a party of my bondsmen (the believers) who used to

say, "O our Lord! We have Imān, so forgive us and show mercy on us. Indeed, You are the best of those who show mercy. But (instead of following their example) you ridiculed (laughed at) them until they (your preoccupation with mocking them) made you forget to remember (worship) Me and you used to (even) laugh (mock) at them. (However, they had patiently endured your taunts and) I have rewarded them today for their patience, (and as a result) they are certainly successful (and will therefore enter Jannah where they will live forever)." (23:108-111)

On the Day of Judgement, the tables will be turned against the disbelievers and the superiority of the believers will be manifest. Whereas the disbelievers laughed at the believers in this world, "however today (on the Day Judgement) the believers shall laugh at the disbelievers while looking on from couches. The fact is that the disbelievers are only punished for what they did." They shall have a taste of their own medicine.

May Allāh ﷻ bless us with His vision on the Day of Judgement in Paradise. Āmeen, Yā Rabbal-Ālameen!!

Other titles from JKN Publications

Your Questions Answered

An outstanding book written by Shaykh Mufti Saiful Islām. A very comprehensive yet simple Fatāwa book and a source of guidance that reaches out to a wider audience i.e. the English speaking Muslims. The reader will benefit from the various answers to questions based on the Laws of Islām relating to the beliefs of Islām, knowledge, Sunnah, pillars of Islām, marriage, divorce and contemporary issues.

UK RRP: £7.50

Hadeeth for Beginners

A concise Hadeeth book with various Ahādeeth that relate to basic Ibādāh and moral etiquettes in Islām accessible to a wider readership. Each Hadeeth has been presented with the Arabic text, its translation and commentary to enlighten the reader, its meaning and application in day-to-day life.

UK RRP: £3.00

Du'ā for Beginners

This book contains basic Du'ās which every Muslim should recite on a daily basis. Highly recommended to young children and adults studying at Islamic schools and Madrasahs so that one may cherish the beautiful treasure of supplications of our beloved Prophet ﷺ in one's daily life, which will ultimately bring peace and happiness in both worlds, Inshā-Allāh.

UK RRP: £2.00

How well do you know Islām?

An exciting educational book which contains 300 multiple questions and answers to help you increase your knowledge on Islām! Ideal for the whole family, especially children and adult students to learn new knowledge in an enjoyable way and cherish the treasures of knowledge that you will acquire from this book. A very beneficial tool for educational syllabus.

UK RRP: £3.00

Treasures of the Holy Qur'ān

This book entitled "Treasures of the Holy Qur'ān" has been compiled to create a stronger bond between the Holy Qur'ān and the readers. It mentions the different virtues of Sūrahs and verses from the Holy Qur'ān with the hope that the readers will increase their zeal and enthusiasm to recite and inculcate the teachings of the Holy Qur'ān into their daily lives.

UK RRP: £3.00

Other titles from JKN PUBLICATIONS

Marriage - A Complete Solution

Islām regards marriage as a great act of worship. This book has been designed to provide the fundamental teachings and guidelines of all what relates to the marital life in a simplified English language. It encapsulates in a nutshell all the marriage laws mentioned in many of the main reference books in order to facilitate their understanding and implementation.

UK RRP: £5.00

Pearls of Luqmān

This book is a comprehensive commentary of Sūrah Luqmān, written beautifully by Shaykh Mufti Saiful Islām. It offers the reader with an enquiring mind, abundance of advice, guidance, counselling and wisdom.

The reader will be enlightened by many wonderful topics and anecdotes mentioned in this book, which will create a greater understanding of the Holy Qur'ān and its wisdom. The book highlights some of the wise sayings and words of advice Luqmān ﷺ gave to his son.

UK RRP: £3.00

Arabic Grammar for Beginners

This book is a study of Arabic Grammar based on the subject of Nahw (Syntax) in a simplified English format. If a student studies this book thoroughly, he/she will develop a very good foundation in this field, Inshā-Allāh. Many books have been written on this subject in various languages such as Arabic, Persian and Urdu. However, in this day and age there is a growing demand for this subject to be available in English .

UK RRP: £3.00

A Gift to My Youngsters

This treasure filled book, is a collection of Islamic stories, morals and anecdotes from the life of our beloved Prophet ﷺ, his Companions ﷺ and the pious predecessors. The stories and anecdotes are based on moral and ethical values, which the reader will enjoy sharing with their peers, friends, families and loved ones.

"A Gift to My Youngsters" – is a wonderful gift presented to the readers personally, by the author himself, especially with the youngsters in mind. He has carefully selected stories and anecdotes containing beautiful morals, lessons and valuable knowledge and wisdom.

UK RRP: £5.00

Travel Companion

The beauty of this book is that it enables a person on any journey, small or distant or simply at home, to utilise their spare time to read and benefit from an exciting and vast collection of important and interesting Islamic topics and lessons. Written in simple and easy to read text, this book will immensely benefit both the newly interested person in Islām and the inquiring mind of a student expanding upon their existing knowledge. Inspiring reminders from the Holy Qur'ān and the blessed words of our beloved Prophet ﷺ beautifies each topic and will illuminate the heart of the reader.   **UK RRP: £5.00**

Pearls of Wisdom

Junaid Baghdādi ﷺ once said, "Allāh ﷻ strengthens through these Islamic stories the hearts of His friends, as proven from the Qur'anic verse,
"And all that We narrate unto you of the stories of the Messengers, so as to strengthen through it your heart." (11:120)
Mālik Ibn Dinār ﷺ stated that such stories are gifts from Paradise. He also emphasised to narrate these stories as much as possible as they are gems and it is possible that an individual might find a truly rare and invaluable gem among them.   **UK RRP: £6.00**

Inspirations

This book contains a compilation of selected speeches delivered by Shaykh Mufti Saiful Islam on a variety of topics such as the Holy Qur'ān, Nikāh and eating Halāl. Having previously been compiled in separate booklets, it was decided that the transcripts be gathered together in one book for the benefit of the reader. In addition to this, we have included in this book, further speeches which have not yet been printed.

UK RRP: £6.00

Gift to my Sisters

A thought provoking compilation of very interesting articles including real life stories of pious predecessors, imaginative illustrations and much more. All designed to influence and motivate mothers, sisters, wives and daughters towards an ideal Islamic lifestyle. A lifestyle referred to by our Creator, Allāh ﷻ in the Holy Qur'ān as the means to salvation and ultimate success.

UK RRP: £6.00

Gift to my Brothers

A thought provoking compilation of very interesting articles including real life stories of pious predecessors, imaginative illustrations, medical advices on intoxicants and rehabilitation and much more. All designed to influence and motivate fathers, brothers, husbands and sons towards an ideal Islamic lifestyle. A lifestyle referred to by our Creator, Allāh ﷻ in the Holy Qur'ān as the means to salvation and ultimate success.

UK RRP: £5.00

Heroes of Islām

"In the narratives there is certainly a lesson for people of intelligence (understanding)." (12:111)

A fine blend of Islamic personalities who have been recognised for leaving a lasting mark in the hearts and minds of people.

A distinguishing feature of this book is that the author has selected not only some of the most world and historically famous renowned scholars but also these lesser known and a few who have simply left behind a valuable piece of advice to their nearest and dearest.   **UK RRP: £5.00**

Ask a Mufti (3 volumes)

Muslims in every generation have confronted different kinds of challenges. In-spite of that, Islām produced such luminary Ulamā who confronted and re-sponded to the challenges of their time to guide the Ummah to the straight path. "Ask A Mufti" is a comprehensive three volume fatwa book, based on the Hanafi School, covering a wide range of topics related to every aspect of human life such as belief, ritual worship, life after death and contemporary legal topics related to purity, commercial transaction, marriage, divorce, food, cosmetic, laws pertaining to women, Islamic medical ethics and much more.

UK RRP: £30.00

Should I Follow a Madhab?

Taqleed or following one of the four legal schools is not a new phenomenon. Historically, scholars of great calibre and luminaries, each one being a specialist in his own right, were known to have adhered to one of the four legal schools. It is only in the previous century that a minority group emerged advocating a se-vere ban on following one of the four major schools.

This book endeavours to address the topic of Taqleed and elucidates its im-portance and necessity in this day and age. It will also, by the Divine Will of Allāh ﷻ dispel some of the confusion surrounding this topic.   **UK RRP: £5.00**

Advice for the Students of Knowledge

Allāh ﷻ describes divine knowledge in the Holy Qur'ān as a 'Light'. Amongst the qualities of light are purity and guidance. The Holy Prophet ﷺ has clearly ex-plained this concept in many blessed Ahādeeth and has also taught us many supplications in which we ask for beneficial knowledge.

This book is a golden tool for every sincere student of knowledge wishing to mould his/her character and engrain those correct qualities in order to be wor-thy of receiving the great gift of Ilm from Allāh ﷻ.   **UK RRP: £3.00**

Stories for Children

"Stories for Children" - is a wonderful gift presented to the readers personally by the author himself, especially with the young children in mind. The stories are based on moral and ethical values, which the reader will enjoy sharing with their peers, friends, families and loved ones. The aim is to present to the children stories and incidents which contain moral lessons, in order to reform and correct their lives, according to the Holy Qur'ān and Sunnah.

UK RRP: £5.00

Pearls from My Shaykh

This book contains a collection of pearls and inspirational accounts of the Holy Prophet ﷺ, his noble Companions, pious predecessors and some personal accounts and sayings of our well-known contemporary scholar and spiritual guide, Shaykh Mufti Saiful Islām Sāhib. Each anecdote and narrative of the pious predecessors have been written in the way that was narrated by Mufti Saiful Islām Sāhib in his discourses, drawing the specific lessons he intended from telling the story. The accounts from the life of the Shaykh has been compiled by a particular student based on their own experience and personal observation. **UK RRP: £5.00**

Paradise & Hell

This book is a collection of detailed explanation of Paradise and Hell including the state and conditions of its inhabitants. All the details have been taken from various reliable sources. The purpose of its compilation is for the reader to contemplate and appreciate the innumerable favours, rewards, comfort and unlimited luxuries of Paradise and at the same time take heed from the punishment of Hell. Shaykh Mufti Saiful Islām Sāhib has presented this book in a unique format by including the Tafseer and virtues of Sūrah Ar-Rahmān. **UK RRP: £5.00**

Prayers for Forgiveness

Prayers for Forgiveness' is a short compilation of Du'ās in Arabic with English translation and transliteration. This book can be studied after 'Du'ā for Beginners' or as a separate book. It includes twenty more Du'ās which have not been mentioned in the previous Du'ā book. It also includes a section of Du'ās from the Holy Qur'ān and a section from the Ahādeeth. The book concludes with a section mentioning the Ninety-Nine Names of Allāh ﷻ with its translation and transliteration. **UK RRP: £3.00**

Scattered Pearls

This book is a collection of scattered pearls taken from books, magazines, emails and WhatsApp messages. These pearls will hopefully increase our knowledge, wisdom and make us realise the purpose of life. In this book, Mufti Sāhib has included messages sent to him from scholars, friends and colleagues which will be beneficial and interesting for our readers Inshā-Allāh. **UK RRP: £4.00**

Poems of Wisdom

This book is a collection of poems from those who contributed to the Al-Mumin Magazine in the poems section. The Hadeeth mentions "Indeed some form of poems are full of wisdom." The themes of each poem vary between wittiness, thought provocation, moral lessons, emotional to name but a few. The readers will benefit from this immensely and make them ponder over the outlook of life in general.

UK RRP: £4.00

This book is a detailed and informative commentary of the first three Sūrahs of the last Juz namely; Sūrah Naba, Sūrah Nāzi'āt and Sūrah Abasa. These Sūrahs vividly depict the horrific events and scenes of the Great Day in order to warn mankind the end of this world. These Sūrahs are an essential reminder for us all to instil the fear and concern of the Day of Judgement and to detach ourselves from the worldly pleasures. Reading this book allows us to attain the true realization of this world and provides essential advices of how to gain eternal salvation in the Hereafter.

RRP: £5:00

It is necessary that Muslims always strive to better themselves at all times and to free themselves from the destructive maladies. This book focusses on three main spiritual maladies; pride, anger and evil gazes. It explains its root causes and offers some spiritual cures. Many examples from the lives of the pious predecessors are used for inspiration and encouragement for controlling the above three maladies. It is hoped that the purification process of the heart becomes easy once the underlying roots of the above maladies are clearly understood. **UK RRP: £5:00**

This book is a step by step guide on Hajj and Umrah for absolute beginners. Many other additional important rulings (Masāil) have been included that will Insha-Allāh prove very useful for our readers. The book also includes some etiquettes of visiting (Ziyārat) of the Holy Prophet's ﷺ blessed Masjid and his Holy Grave.

UK   RRP   £3:00

This book contains essential guidelines for a spiritual Mureed to gain some familiarity of the science of Tasawwuf. It explains the meaning and aims of Tasawwuf, some understanding around the concept of the soul, and general guidelines for a spiritual Mureed. This is highly recommended book and it is hoped that it gains wider readership among those Mureeds who are basically new to the science of Tasawwuf.

UK RRP £3:00

This book is a compilation of sayings and earnest pieces of advice that have been gathered directly from my respected teacher Shaykh Mufti Saiful Islām Sāhib. The book consists of many valuable enlightenments including how to deal with challenges of life, promoting unity, practicing good manners, being optimistic and many other valuable advices. Our respected Shaykh has gathered this Naseehah from meditating, contemplating, analysing and searching for the gems within Qur'anic verses, Ahādeeth and teachings of our Pious Predecessors. **UK RRP £1:00**

Kanzul Bāri

Kanzul Bāri provides a detailed commentary of the Ahādeeth contained in Saheeh al-Bukhāri. The commentary includes Imām Bukhāri's ﷺ biography, the status of his book, spiritual advice, inspirational accounts along with academic discussions related to Fiqh, its application and differences of opinion. Moreover, it answers objections arising in one's mind about certain Ahādeeth. Inquisitive students of Hadeeth will find this commentary a very useful reference book in the final year of their Ālim course for gaining a deeper understanding of the science of Hadeeth.   **UK RRP: £15.00**

How to Become a Friend of Allāh ﷻ

The friends of Allāh ﷻ have been described in detail in the Holy Qur'ān and Āhadeeth. This book endeavours its readers to help create a bond with Allāh ﷻ in attaining His friendship as He is the sole Creator of all material and immaterial things. It is only through Allāh's ﷻ friendship, an individual will achieve happiness in this life and the Hereafter, hence eliminate worries, sadness, depression, anxiety and misery of this world.   **UK RRP: £3.00**

Gems & Jewels

This book contains a selection of articles which have been gathered for the benefit of the readers covering a variety of topics on various aspects of daily life. It offers precious advice and anecdotes that contain moral lessons. The advice captivates its readers and will extend the narrowness of their thoughts to deep reflection, wisdom and appreciation of the purpose of our existence.

UK RRP: £4.00

End of Time

This book is a comprehensive explanation of the three Sūrahs of Juzz Amma; Sūrah Takweer, Sūrah Infitār and Sūrah Mutaffifeen. This book is a continuation from the previous book of the same author, 'Horrors of Judgement Day'. The three Sūrahs vividly sketch out the scene of the Day of Judgement and describe the state of both the inmates of Jannah and Jahannam. Mufti Saiful Islām Sāhib provides an easy but comprehensive commentary of the three Sūrahs facilitating its understanding for the readers whilst capturing the horrific scene of the ending of the world and the conditions of mankind on that horrific Day.   **UK RRP: £5.00**